MISSIONPRENEUR MINDSET:

LEGACY & GENERATIONAL LEADERSHIP

Building Faith, Family, and Kingdom Impact That Outlives You

Table of Contents

ACKNOWLEDGMENTS

To everyone who has been part of my journey—this book is as much yours as it is mine.

To my family, who has believed in the mission even on the days it required sacrifice—thank you. Your unwavering support has grounded me and strengthened me in ways no professional success ever could. You are not merely appreciated; you are the foundation upon which everything else stands. You remain my greatest blessing and my fiercest motivation through every challenge.

To the mentors, leaders, and coaches who invested in me long before there were stages, chapters, or microphones—your impact cannot be overstated. Thank you for pushing me when I needed it, challenging me when I resisted growth, and recognizing potential in me when I couldn't yet see it in myself. Your wisdom, correction, and belief are intricately woven into every page of this book.

To the athletes, entrepreneurs, leaders, and world-changers I've had the privilege of teaching, coaching, learning from, and walking alongside—you continually remind me why this mission matters. Your relentless hunger to grow, your steadfast refusal to settle, and your openness to development fuel everything I build and share with the world.

To the students and young dreamers who reach out with messages, questions, ideas, and boldly spoken goals—you inspire me more than you could possibly know. Your passion is truly the future. Because you choose to pursue calling instead of comfort, generations that follow will reap the benefits of your courage.

To the readers of my books—whether this is your first or one of many—I am deeply grateful for your trust. You've entrusted me with your time, attention, and personal growth journey. Through this exchange, you allow my calling to fulfill its purpose: to multiply greatness in others.

To every person who has prayed for me, encouraged me, challenged me, corrected me, sharpened me, or even disagreed with me—thank you for your contribution. True growth rarely happens in comfort zones, and I am better because of your influence in my life.

And finally, to the One who gave me breath, assignment, and purpose—I acknowledge that none of this is possible without Your grace. Thank You for the calling, the strength, the lessons, the pressure, the victories, the refinement, and the sacred responsibility to serve others through what You have planted in me. My deepest prayer is that every word written here ultimately points back to You through the lives it touches and transforms.

If this book impacts you in any way, then every season, every lesson, and every test that shaped it was profoundly worth it.

Thank you for being part of this continuing mission.

INTRODUCTION

Why Missionpreneur Legacy Matters

This book was not born out of theory. It was forged through responsibility and years of hands-on leadership experience.

For years, I lived in the same tension many leaders know intimately—building organizations, leading teams, coaching athletes, growing institutions, and carrying vision that consistently felt larger than a single season of life. Success brought momentum. Momentum brought opportunity. Opportunity inevitably brought complexity.

And complexity exposed a sobering truth:

Success can be built quickly.

Legacy cannot.

Legacy requires intention, structure, humility, and faith. It cannot be improvised or assumed. Most importantly, it cannot depend on one person's vision or energy forever.

When Building Became Stewarding

The pivotal shift began when leadership evolved from being about expansion to becoming about guardianship. This transformation fundamentally changed everything.

The questions transformed.

No longer just:

- How big can this become?
- How fast can we scale?
- How much can we accomplish?

But deeper, more consequential questions emerged:

- What survives if I'm not here?
- Who is being intentionally prepared to lead next?
- What values are embedded deeply enough to endure pressure, transition, and the test of time?

These questions did not originate in boardrooms or strategy sessions. They surfaced in family conversations, moments of accountability, seasons of stretching, and quiet prayer.

Eventually, they led to the intentional formation of Angeron and Melvin Legacy Holdings, LLC—a structure designed to address these critical questions.

Why Angeron and Melvin Legacy Holdings Exists

Angeron and Melvin Legacy Holdings was not created primarily as a financial vehicle. It was established as a legacy framework—a deliberate architecture for sustainable impact.

A structure designed to:

♦ Align faith, family, and enterprise in harmonious purpose

♦ Separate ownership from authority with clear boundaries

♦ Codify values before scale compromises them

♦ Create clarity instead of confusion across generations

♦ Protect future generations from today's shortcuts and compromises

This decision forced me to confront uncomfortable realities that many leaders avoid:

♦ Vision alone is insufficient without implementation

♦ Good intentions do not replace proper governance

♦ Love without structure creates organizational fragility

♦ Silence today inevitably becomes conflict tomorrow

Forming a holding company was not simply a business move. It was a profound leadership reckoning that demanded honest self-assessment.

It required moving from being the center of everything to becoming a steward of systems—systems thoughtfully designed to function with or without my presence.

From Entrepreneur to Missionpreneur

Entrepreneurs build for opportunity. Missionpreneurs build for assignment and purpose.

Entrepreneurs ask, "What can I do?"

Missionpreneurs ask, "What am I called to steward?"

That distinction fundamentally changed everything about our approach to business and legacy.

It transformed how decisions were made. It revolutionized how family was prioritized. It redefined how succession was discussed and planned. It completely reshaped how leadership was trained, developed, and released.

Missionpreneur leadership demanded:

♦ That faith govern decisions—not merely decorate them

♦ That family be intentionally organized—not casually assumed

♦ That systems outlive personalities and individual charisma

♦ That succession be planned and implemented—not perpetually postponed

And most importantly, it demanded genuine humility—the willingness to admit that what I built could not and should not depend on me forever.

Why This Book Exists

This book exists because too many visionary leaders:

♦ Win publicly and fracture privately in unseen ways

♦ Grow quickly and collapse later under unsustainable structures

♦ Build platforms but not capable successors

♦ Leave financial inheritance without proper preparation

I have watched ministries struggle profoundly after founders step away. I have seen thriving businesses weaken dramatically during leadership transitions. I have witnessed families divide bitterly over silence that could have been addressed early through proper communication.

None of that happens overnight or by accident.

It happens slowly, incrementally—when legacy is passively assumed instead of actively designed with intention.

This book is a direct response to that pervasive reality.

What This Book Is — and Is Not

This is not a motivational book. It is a construction manual for building lasting impact.

It is not about charisma or personality. It is about continuity and sustainable systems.

It is not anti-growth or against expansion. It is pro-alignment and focused on integrity.

Every chapter was written from lived experience—through leadership pressure, family responsibility, institutional building, and the demanding work of putting proper governance around compelling vision.

What you will read has been tested in real decisions, real conversations, and real consequences—not theoretical scenarios.

Who This Book Is For

This book is specifically designed for:

- Leaders who recognize their influence must outlive their direct involvement
- Entrepreneurs transitioning from growth-focused to governance-focused leadership
- Parents committed to preparing the next generation intentionally
- Founders beginning to thoughtfully consider succession planning
- Faith-driven leaders who refuse to separate spiritual calling from organizational construction

If you are content with short-term success and immediate results, this book may frustrate you. If you are committed to building faithful legacy that spans generations, it will challenge you in necessary ways.

The Missionpreneur Invitation

This book will not ask you to build bigger empires. It will ask you to build deeper foundations that can sustain meaningful impact.

It will ask you to honestly examine:

- Where vision lives only in your head instead of being properly documented
- Where systems are missing or insufficient for future growth
- Where family clarity is overdue and conversations have been avoided
- Where obedience must replace ambition in your leadership journey

And it will invite you to make peace with a final truth:

You may never fully see the complete impact of what you build—

but generations will live inside the legacy you construct today.

A Final Word Before You Begin

Legacy is not something you passively leave behind at the end of your journey. It is something you actively construct daily— through consistent decisions, disciplined practices, faith-filled choices, and genuine humility.

Angeron and Melvin Legacy Holdings, LLC was one tangible expression of that commitment. This book represents another step in that ongoing mission.

My sincere prayer is that what follows helps you move from being the center of the mission

to becoming its strongest, most enduring foundation.

Because when leaders build well enough to eventually disappear,

the mission finally becomes strong enough to endure beyond any single individual.

Let's begin this journey together.

CHAPTER 1

THE CALL (WHY LEGACY MATTERS)

Most people believe legacy is something you leave behind. This perspective treats legacy as a distant afterthought, something to consider only after success has been achieved or retirement approaches. Many leaders operate under this misconception, postponing critical decisions that shape their lasting impact.

Scripture teaches something far more sobering. The biblical perspective reveals legacy as an active, ongoing responsibility rather than a passive outcome. Throughout both Old and New Testaments, we see leadership portrayed not merely as present influence but as generational stewardship.

Legacy is something you are actively building—whether you intend to or not. Every decision you make is shaping what survives you. Every value you model is being transferred, reinforced, or distorted. Every system you build—or refuse to build—determines whether what you stewarded will multiply or quietly collapse. The infrastructure you establish today creates the framework for tomorrow's continuation or collapse.

Legacy is not optional.

Only intention is.

Leadership carries weight far beyond the moment. It reaches into futures you may never see and into lives you may never personally touch. That reality makes legacy one of the most misunderstood—and most avoided—subjects in leadership today. Yet ignoring legacy does not delay its impact; it simply forfeits control of it. When leaders fail to intentionally shape their legacy, they don't prevent one from forming—they merely surrender its direction to chance, circumstance, or others' interpretations.

The Dangerous Myth of "Someday"

One of the great deceptions of leadership is the belief that legacy is a future concern. It sounds reasonable on the surface: I'll think about succession later. I'll deal with legacy once things stabilize. Right now, I just need to survive. This thinking creates an artificial separation between present leadership and future impact, suggesting that the two operate independently.

Survival mode is understandable. Many leaders step into responsibility during crisis, pressure, or uncertainty. The immediate demands of stabilizing operations, meeting payroll, or navigating market disruptions can consume every available moment and resource. These pressing concerns often feel more urgent than legacy planning.

But leaders who remain in survival mode too long unintentionally create fragility for everyone else. What begins as adaptability turns into avoidance. What begins as focus becomes tunnel vision. Teams learn to respond only to emergencies rather than build for sustainability. Organizations develop reactive cultures instead of proactive systems. The very adaptability that helped navigate initial challenges becomes an obstacle to long-term stability.

The truth, though uncomfortable, is unavoidable. If you are leading anything—a family, a business, a team, a ministry—you are already writing your legacy. The only question is whether you are writing it by design or by default. Every policy you implement, every hire you make, every culture you foster is creating patterns that will outlast your direct involvement. These patterns become the operating system others inherit.

Default leadership produces short-term wins but long-term instability. Intentional leadership builds with the future in view, even when the present feels demanding. Legacy thinking does not wait for the perfect moment; it begins in imperfect seasons. It recognizes that today's decisions create tomorrow's foundation, regardless of whether those decisions were made with legacy in mind.

Success Is Not the End Game

Culture celebrates success. God examines stewardship. This fundamental distinction separates leadership that impresses from leadership that endures. Our business culture particularly glorifies rapid growth, market dominance, and personal achievement, often at the expense of sustainability and transferability.

Success measures growth, scale, and visible results. Legacy measures durability, transferability, and faithfulness beyond the original leader. Success asks whether something expanded. Legacy asks whether it can endure without you. Success focuses on what can be counted; legacy focuses on what can be continued.

Many leaders succeed brilliantly and fail generationally. They build impressive platforms but neglect to develop people. They create income streams but leave no inheritance of values, vision, or responsibility. Their organizations grow dependent on their presence rather than strengthened by their leadership. When they step away—whether through retirement, transition, or unexpected circumstances—what appeared robust often reveals structural weakness.

If your leadership cannot be transferred, it remains incomplete. If everything depends on your personality, charisma, or constant oversight, you haven't built a system—you've built a bottleneck. Legacy leadership requires more than momentum; it requires preparation. It demands the humility to build processes that others can operate, document wisdom that others can access, and cultivate values that others can embody even when you're not present.

Legacy Is a Responsibility Before It Is a Reward

Legacy is often romanticized as something recognized after death—plaques, tributes, stories retold by others. This perspective treats legacy as primarily reputational, focusing on how one is remembered rather than what one leaves functional. Many leaders inadvertently pursue memorial-building rather than mission-sustaining.

Scripture presents a far more demanding picture. Biblical legacy is rooted in responsibility, not recognition. It is measured by obedience over time, not applause in the moment. Abraham did not simply receive a promise; he accepted an assignment that extended beyond his lifetime. David did not merely defeat giants; he prepared resources for a temple he would never personally build. Jesus did not lead crowds for admiration; He formed disciples to carry the mission forward after His departure.

In God's economy, legacy is never accidental. It is the fruit of faithful stewardship practiced consistently, often quietly, and sometimes without visible reward. This stewardship encompasses resources, relationships, knowledge, and opportunities—all viewed not as personal possessions but as entrusted assets meant to benefit future generations.

Biblical Example: David and the Legacy He Would Never See

King David stands as one of the clearest examples of intentional legacy leadership. Though he was chosen as king, victorious in battle, and celebrated by the people, David understood that not everything God placed in his heart would be fulfilled through his own hands. His leadership maturity is revealed not in what he accomplished personally, but in how he prepared what would outlast him.

God made it clear that David would not build the temple. Instead of resisting that limitation or pursuing recognition anyway, David shifted his focus. He gathered resources. He organized materials. He prepared plans. He instructed his son. Scripture records that David gave Solomon detailed direction, not only about construction but about faithfulness, obedience, and leadership.

David's legacy was not built in the moment he passed authority to Solomon. It was built in the years he spent preparing someone else to carry forward what mattered most. That is the distinction between successful leaders and legacy leaders. One accumulates. The other equips. One builds monuments to personal achievement; the other builds mechanisms for ongoing impact.

David teaches us that legacy leadership requires humility—the willingness to build something that someone else will complete, steward, and sometimes receive credit for. This humility doesn't diminish the leader's importance; rather, it magnifies their impact by extending it beyond their direct control. David's fingerprints remained on the temple he never saw constructed because he prioritized preparation over personal recognition.

Why Most Leaders Avoid Legacy Thinking

Legacy thinking forces honest self-examination. It raises questions many leaders would rather postpone. What happens if I am no longer here? Have I built people or merely dependence? Do my values exist in writing, or only in my head? Would those closest to me describe my leadership the same way I do? These questions demand vulnerability and expose gaps between intention and implementation.

These questions expose uncomfortable realities. They surface control issues, ego attachments, fear of replacement, and unresolved family or organizational tension. Many leaders avoid legacy planning not because they are careless, but because legacy reveals what they have postponed confronting. The mirror of legacy reflects not just achievements but deficiencies, not just strengths but succession gaps.

Avoidance, however, never eliminates consequences. What leaders delay today often becomes division tomorrow. Unaddressed succession questions create uncertainty. Undocumented processes become operational vulnerabilities. Unspoken expectations lead to misalignment. The very issues leaders avoid addressing eventually undermine what they've worked so hard to build.

The Missionpreneur Distinction

A Missionpreneur does not ask how big something can get. A Missionpreneur asks how far it can go beyond them. This fundamental reframing transforms every aspect of building, from strategic planning to team development to operational design. It shifts the measurement of success from personal achievement to transferable impact.

This distinction changes everything. Missionpreneurs build with the next generation in mind. They understand that charisma fades, but systems transfer. Values must be codified, not assumed. Leadership must be multiplied, not centralized. Their decisions reflect a commitment to longevity over celebrity and sustainability over temporary advantage.

Missionpreneurs do not merely pursue success; they intentionally build successors. They refuse to confuse growth with maturity or visibility with sustainability. Their leadership is measured not by how many follow them, but by how many can lead after them. This approach requires investing disproportionately in people development, knowledge transfer, and systematic documentation—activities that rarely make headlines but ultimately determine legacy.

When Legacy Quietly Leaks

Legacy rarely collapses all at once. More often, it erodes silently when one domain is neglected. Faith becomes private but disconnected from operational decisions. Family conversations remain unspoken while business documentation receives meticulous attention. Authority becomes over-centralized while delegation is verbally championed. Multiplication is assumed rather than practiced through intentional mentoring and release of responsibility.

You cannot outsource legacy, and you cannot compensate for a broken foundation with public success. Strength in one area cannot permanently mask neglect in another. Faith, family, enterprise, and multiplication must remain aligned for legacy to endure. When these domains fall out of alignment, the resulting tension creates fractures that widen over time, eventually compromising even the strongest structures.

A Sobering Question

Every Missionpreneur must face this question—early, honestly, and often: If I stepped away today, would what I've built grow stronger or struggle to survive? This question strips away pretense and reveals the true state of your leadership infrastructure. It distinguishes between organizations built around a person and organizations built around a purpose.

This is not a pessimistic question. It is a responsible one. Strong legacy builders are not threatened by this evaluation; they use it as a compass. It recalibrates priorities and clarifies what needs strengthening before it's too late. It exposes dependencies that require attention and highlights processes that need documentation or simplification to function without the founder's constant oversight.

From Intention to Action

Legacy does not begin with a will. It begins with alignment. This book will not ask you to build monuments. It will challenge you to build structures. Not louder platforms, but deeper foundations. Not famous moments, but faithful systems. These structures include clear values, documented processes, intentional development pathways, and sustainable operational models that can function beyond the founder's daily involvement.

Legacy is not something you leave behind someday. It is something you steward—starting now. Today's decisions create tomorrow's reality. The conversations you initiate, the documentation you create, the leaders you develop, and the values you reinforce are all active legacy-building work. This intentionality transforms leadership from temporary influence to generational impact.

Reflection Questions

1. In what areas of my leadership am I relying too heavily on my own presence rather than transferable systems? Which processes would falter if I were unavailable for 30 days?

2. What values matter most to me, and where are they clearly documented, taught, or modeled? How would I know if these values were being diluted or misinterpreted?

3. Who could step into my role today, even temporarily, and what gaps would be exposed? What specific knowledge or relationships exist only in my head?

4. Where have I postponed legacy conversations because they feel uncomfortable? What specific conversations about succession, authority transfer, or future vision have I avoided?

5. What would faithfulness look like if recognition and results were removed? How would my leadership priorities change if no one knew what I accomplished?

Closing Declaration

I was not called to build something merely impressive.

I was called to build something enduring.

I accept the responsibility of stewardship over ownership.

I will lead with obedience, not ego, and alignment over adrenaline.

I will build systems that serve people, develop leaders, and honor God.

What God entrusts to me will not end with me.

I am intentional.

I am accountable.

I am committed to generational impact.

I am a Missionpreneur, and I build for legacy.

Chapter 2

Built for More

Why the Mission Matters More Than the Moment

Somewhere inside every high performer—athlete, entrepreneur, leader, coach, parent, or creative—there is a quiet voice that never fully goes away. This voice persists through success and failure, through celebration and disappointment. It speaks with clarity even when circumstances cloud your vision. This internal compass points toward your true potential, not just your current reality.

You were built for more.

You don't always feel it. You don't always believe it. Some days, you can't even define what more means yet. But it remains—steady, persistent, and undeniable—because it is not ambition whispering to you. It is calling. This distinction is crucial for sustainable achievement and meaningful impact in both business and life.

You were not created for an average life. You were not wired to blend in, settle, or shrink your impact to stay comfortable. There is something within you that refuses mediocrity, even when circumstances try to convince you otherwise. This refusal to settle is the foundation upon which legacy businesses, transformative leadership, and generational impact are built.

Yet most people never become who they were created to be. Not because they lack desire, talent, or opportunity—but because they were never taught how to think, live, and lead from purpose. The gap between potential and fulfillment is rarely about capability and almost always about identity, mindset, and alignment with deeper calling.

The world is excellent at developing skill but poor at developing identity. Schools sharpen talent. Coaches refine technique. Culture rewards comparison. Social media amplifies attention. But very few environments teach people how to carry the weight of calling without collapsing under it—how to lead when no one is watching, how to stay disciplined without burning out, how to thrive mentally, spiritually, physically, and emotionally, and how to build a life strong enough to sustain greatness. These foundations are essential for those who wish to create lasting impact through their business endeavors.

That gap is where most potential dies.

You Don't Need More Motivation—You Need a Mission

Motivation is loud, emotional, and temporary. It gets you started, but it rarely gets you through adversity. Mission is quieter, deeper, and far more powerful. Mission doesn't hype you—it anchors you. When market conditions shift, when competition intensifies, when personal challenges arise, motivation fades but mission remains.

Mission-driven people don't perform to impress. They perform to fulfill what they were created to do. They don't build confidence on applause or comparison; they build it on identity. They don't live from emotion; they live from assignment. This mindset transforms how you approach business decisions, leadership challenges, and long-term strategy.

When someone lives mission-first, their leadership stabilizes. Focus becomes consistent. Discipline becomes normal. Pressure no longer feels like punishment but confirmation that they are operating at the level they were designed for. Setbacks become teachers instead of threats. Success becomes repeatable rather than fragile. These qualities are precisely what distinguish enduring enterprises from fleeting ventures.

The goal of this book is not to make you excited. Excitement fades. The goal is to make you unshakable. Market volatility, economic uncertainty, and competitive pressures test every business owner and leader. Those who build from mission rather than momentum develop the resilience to withstand these tests.

Why This Book Exists

You do not need another motivational speech. You need a transformation in the way you think about pressure, identity, discipline, and purpose. This transformation will fundamentally alter how you approach business development, team leadership, strategic planning, and personal growth.

Most people never reach their full potential because the internal structure they are living with cannot support the level of greatness they are chasing. They try to build high-impact lives on weak mental and emotional foundations. They grind harder instead of aligning deeper. Eventually, pressure exposes what preparation did not reinforce. This principle applies equally to individual leaders and organizational cultures.

You were not designed to crumble under pressure. You were not designed to grind until you break. You were not designed to chase affirmation just to feel worthy. You were designed to build a life that turns calling into legacy. This perspective shifts how you measure success, allocate resources, and create value in the marketplace.

That requires a mindset the world does not teach—a Missionpreneur mindset. This mindset integrates purpose with performance, values with vision, and calling with commerce in ways that traditional business education often overlooks.

What Is a Missionpreneur?

A Missionpreneur is not merely a high performer. A Missionpreneur is a called performer. This distinction fundamentally changes how decisions are made, priorities are set, and resources are allocated. It transforms the metrics of success from purely financial to deeply purposeful.

A Missionpreneur builds life around purpose rather than attention. Pressure is not viewed as proof of inadequacy but as evidence of assignment. Gifts are used to elevate others, not inflate ego. Integrity is not negotiable, even when opportunity tempts compromise. These principles create a foundation for ethical leadership and sustainable business practices.

Missionpreneurs understand that success without alignment is unsustainable. They do not chase success; they steward calling until success becomes inevitable. They finish well, not just fast. This long-term perspective influences everything from financial planning to succession strategy to legacy development.

A Missionpreneur lives by assignment, not emotion. And assignment gives meaning to every sacrifice required along the way. This clarity of purpose transforms obstacles into opportunities and challenges into catalysts for growth and innovation.

Biblical Example: Joseph—Built Before He Was Positioned

Joseph's life is one of the clearest biblical examples of someone who was built for more long before he was positioned for more. As a young man, Joseph carried a God-given vision, but he lacked the maturity to hold its weight. Betrayal, rejection, false accusation, and imprisonment followed—not because God had abandoned him, but because God was preparing him. This preparation process holds powerful lessons for modern entrepreneurs facing adversity.

Joseph was promoted internally before he was promoted publicly. His character was refined in obscurity. His integrity was tested in temptation. His leadership was proven without recognition. By the time opportunity arrived, Joseph did not need hype to step into purpose—he was already formed. This pattern of private development preceding public deployment applies directly to business leadership today.

Joseph teaches us this critical truth: calling precedes clarity, and preparation often looks like delay. You may feel overlooked, underutilized, or misunderstood, but that does not mean you are behind. It may mean you are being built for the weight of what is coming. This perspective transforms how we interpret business challenges, market setbacks, and personal disappointments.

A Mindset That Can Handle Greatness

This book is a manual for the mind, a framework for identity, and a blueprint for sustainable impact. Not surface-level success, but greatness that does not destroy you in the process. It addresses both the external metrics of achievement and the internal foundations that make those achievements meaningful and sustainable.

As you move through these chapters, you will learn how to stop chasing approval and start operating from calling; how to turn pressure into performance; how to build confidence that doesn't collapse under adversity; how to use purpose as your competitive advantage; how to develop discipline without burnout; and how to build a life strong enough to support both success and legacy. These principles apply equally to personal leadership and organizational culture.

This is not a book about feeling good. It is a book about becoming great—the kind of greatness your soul, family, and future can sustain. It addresses the holistic nature of true success, integrating business achievement with personal fulfillment and relational health.

Stretch Is Part of Becoming

Some chapters will fuel you. Others will confront you. Growth is not always comfortable, but it is always necessary. This book will challenge mental patterns that have limited you, silence internal voices that sabotage you, and help you build habits that stabilize rather than exhaust you. These transformations are essential for both personal leadership and organizational development.

If you lean in, you will not finish this book the same person who started it—because you were never meant to. The principles contained here will reshape not only how you think about business but how you approach your entire life's work and purpose.

You Are Not Behind—You Are Becoming

Maybe you wish you had learned these principles earlier. Maybe you feel as though time, opportunity, or potential has been wasted. Release that weight now. This perspective shift is crucial for moving forward with clarity and confidence rather than regret and hesitation.

You are not late—you are being developed. Pressure did not break you; it revealed where reinforcement was needed. Failure did not disqualify you; it sharpened wisdom. Delay did not deny destiny; it prepared you to handle it. These reframings transform how you interpret past business challenges and personal setbacks.

You are not behind.

You are in training.

And now you are ready for what comes next. This readiness positions you to approach new opportunities with wisdom, resilience, and purpose rather than merely ambition, anxiety, or attachment to outcomes.

Reflection Questions

1. Where in my life have I mistaken motivation for mission? How has this affected my business decisions and leadership approach?

2. What pressure am I currently facing that may actually be preparation? How might this reframing change my response to current challenges?

3. How secure is my identity when recognition is absent? How does this impact my leadership during difficult business seasons?

4. What areas of my life need greater alignment before greater opportunity? Which misalignments pose the greatest risk to sustainable success?

5. Am I building a life strong enough to support the level of impact I desire? What foundations need strengthening to sustain the growth I envision?

Closing Declaration

I was built for more—but not more noise, more pressure, or more approval.

I was built for purpose.

I choose mission over moment and calling over comparison.

I will not rush what God is still forming.

I will steward my gifts with discipline, integrity, and patience.

Pressure will refine me, not define me.

My life will be strong enough to carry the weight of destiny.

I am not chasing success.

I am fulfilling assignment.

I am a Missionpreneur, and I was built for more.

CHAPTER 3

STOP CHASING, START CALLING

The Difference Between Goals and Mission

Adrenaline makes you fast.

Calling makes you consistent.

We live in a world that glorifies the grind—the hustle, the race, the highlight reel. People are taught to chase goals, applause, titles, statistics, money, and validation as if those things will finally make them feel whole. The chase is celebrated so loudly that we've forgotten a dangerous truth: success without purpose is merely motion without meaning. The entrepreneurial landscape is littered with burned-out achievers who conquered everything except fulfillment.

You can pursue everything the world tells you to want and still miss what you were created to do. This misalignment represents the greatest hidden cost in business today—talented individuals directing their energy toward objectives that never belonged to them in the first place. As missionpreneurs, we must recognize that our greatest competitive advantage isn't speed, but sustainability through alignment.

"Follow your dreams" sounds inspiring, but it raises a critical question: what if the dream isn't even yours? What if it was inherited from culture, borrowed from someone else's expectations, or shaped by fear, comparison, or insecurity? What if you're running at full speed in the wrong direction? The marketplace rewards authenticity precisely because it has become so rare—most entrepreneurs are chasing someone else's definition of success.

Most people don't fail because they're lazy.

They fail because they're misaligned.

They're climbing quickly, but the ladder is leaning against the wrong wall. This misplacement of energy creates an unsustainable business model where effort never translates to fulfillment. When we build enterprises based on external validation rather than internal calling, we construct businesses that drain rather than energize us.

When Motivation Isn't Enough

Motivation can get you started, but it has limits. Eventually, applause fades, progress slows, fatigue sets in, doubt creeps in, and life pushes back harder than expected. That is the moment most people unravel—not because they lack talent or effort, but because they were running on adrenaline instead of assignment. The sustainability of our business ventures depends not on initial enthusiasm but on the alignment between our operations and our purpose.

Adrenaline thrives on excitement and emotion. Assignment thrives on clarity and purpose. Adrenaline delivers moments; assignment builds a life. You don't become unstoppable through hype. You become unstoppable through alignment. This principle applies equally to individual entrepreneurs and established organizations—the entities with longevity are those whose missions transcend market fluctuations.

When effort is fueled only by emotion, consistency disappears as soon as emotion fluctuates. But when effort is rooted in calling, discipline no longer depends on how you feel—it flows from who you know you are. This identity-based performance creates resilient business models capable of weathering economic uncertainty, competitive pressure, and the inevitable challenges of entrepreneurship.

Biblical Example: David and the Power of Assignment

The story of David and Goliath is often framed as an underdog victory, but at its core, it is a study in alignment. Every soldier on the battlefield saw the same giant. They calculated the same risk. They felt the same fear. Yet one young shepherd stepped forward without hesitation. In business terms, David recognized an opportunity others perceived as a threat because he operated from a different framework—one based on calling rather than conventional wisdom.

David wasn't responding to adrenaline or applause. He wasn't chasing a moment. He was fulfilling an assignment. His confidence came not from overestimating his abilities but from understanding his purpose. Similarly, missionpreneurs distinguish themselves by pursuing opportunities aligned with their calling rather than following market trends that promise quick returns but lack personal resonance.

While everyone else was trying to avoid failure, David was anchored in identity. He knew who he was, whose he was, and what he had been prepared to do. Calling removed confusion, and when confusion disappeared, fear lost its grip. This clarity of purpose represents a competitive advantage in business—decisions become simpler, priorities clearer, and execution more focused when filtered through the lens of assignment.

David teaches us that when you know what you are built for, pressure no longer feels like a threat—it feels like confirmation. The moment didn't create David; it revealed him. Likewise, market challenges don't define missionpreneurs; they reveal the depth of our commitment to purpose over profit and calling over convenience.

The Identity Shift That Changes Everything

Identity is the control center of performance. People who chase goals say, "I want to win." People who live from calling say, "I'm built to do this." That subtle shift transforms everything—confidence, decision-making, emotional control, discipline, resilience, and consistency. This perspective creates business leaders who maintain vision during volatility and stay committed when competitors pivot to chase trends.

That subtle shift transforms everything—confidence, decision-making, emotional control, discipline, resilience, and consistency.

You do not rise to the level of your goals; you rise to the level of who you believe you are. When this principle guides our business development, we build enterprises that reflect our values rather than merely responding to market demands.

If someone believes they succeed only when conditions are favorable, their performance will always depend on ease. But when someone believes they are built to thrive under pressure, pressure becomes fuel rather than fear. Identity anchors effort long after excitement fades. Missionpreneurs understand that sustainable business models emerge from this identity-based approach— creating ventures that energize rather than deplete us.

Why High Achievers Still Feel Empty

It is possible to check every box culture tells you should lead to fulfillment and still feel hollow. External success cannot compensate for internal misalignment. You can earn the money, win the award, receive the title, post the highlight, and still look in the mirror feeling disconnected. This phenomenon explains why many objectively successful entrepreneurs still struggle with dissatisfaction—achievement without alignment creates prosperity without purpose.

Success without calling feels like success without soul. The marketplace is filled with profitable enterprises that provide no fulfillment to their founders because the business model was built on opportunity alone rather than opportunity aligned with calling. When profit becomes the sole metric of success, even financial abundance fails to satisfy.

The world teaches people to chase achievement. Calling teaches people to steward assignment. Assignment is not about status—it is about purpose. When purpose is missing, achievement becomes exhausting rather than energizing. Missionpreneurs measure success differently—not just by financial outcomes but by alignment between business activities and personal calling.

How to Discern Chasing from Calling

One of the clearest indicators of alignment is sustainability without recognition. If applause disappeared, would you still do the work? If validation vanished, would the commitment remain? If the spotlight shifted, would the responsibility still feel internal? These questions reveal whether our business endeavors emerge from authentic calling or mere opportunity.

If the answer depends on attention, it is chasing.

If the answer endures without it, it is calling.

Elite performers don't operate for attention; they operate with attention—attention to detail, growth, discipline, excellence, and preparation. They are grounded in assignment, not affirmation. This distinction creates business leaders who maintain consistent performance regardless of external validation or market recognition. Their commitment to excellence stems from internal standards rather than external metrics.

For missionpreneurs, this principle transforms how we evaluate business opportunities. We filter potential ventures not just through profit potential but through alignment with our calling. This approach may sometimes mean declining lucrative opportunities that don't align with our purpose—a counterintuitive strategy that ultimately creates more sustainable success.

Calling Is Often Quiet Before It Is Clear

Many people wait for a dramatic revelation—a lightning bolt moment that announces their calling. In reality, calling is often subtle. It may arrive as a persistent pull, a restless dissatisfaction with comfort, or a fire you can't fully explain. Sometimes calling is simply the thing you cannot stop thinking about or walk away from. For entrepreneurs, this might manifest as an idea that persists despite logical objections or a market need you feel uniquely positioned to address.

Calling does not always draw applause. It may be misunderstood, questioned, or resisted by others—especially by those who are still chasing. Calling threatens complacency because it exposes misalignment. When we build businesses based on calling rather than convention, we often face skepticism from traditional business thinkers who prioritize immediate returns over long-term alignment.

The journey from identifying calling to building a business model around it requires patience and discernment. What begins as an internal conviction gradually crystallizes into a viable enterprise as we consistently take steps aligned with our purpose. This organic development creates businesses with strong foundations because they emerge from authentic calling rather than manufactured opportunity.

The Psychology Behind Calling-Driven Performance

Performance psychology consistently confirms what Scripture has taught for generations: people perform better under pressure when identity is rooted in purpose rather than outcomes. Calling-driven motivation produces greater resilience, lower burnout, and faster recovery from failure. These psychological advantages translate directly to business performance, creating entrepreneurs who maintain effectiveness during market downturns and competitive challenges.

People fueled by hype collapse when hype fades.

People fueled by calling accelerate when hype disappears.

Intrinsic motivation outlasts emotional momentum. Alignment sustains effort when circumstances fluctuate. This principle explains why some businesses thrive during economic uncertainty while others falter—those built on calling possess a resilience that transcends market conditions. Their commitment doesn't depend on external validation but on internal conviction about their purpose.

For missionpreneurs, this psychological framework transforms how we approach business development. We build enterprises designed for sustainability rather than mere scalability, recognizing that alignment with calling creates natural motivation that outlasts market enthusiasm. This approach produces businesses that energize rather than deplete their founders, even during challenging seasons.

Living From Calling Instead of Chasing

Transformation begins with better questions. Stop asking what will impress people and start asking what feels like assignment. Stop asking what will get attention and start asking what you would regret not doing. When life shifts from chasing goals to fulfilling calling, discipline becomes natural, distractions lose power, emotions stop controlling effort, and confidence stabilizes. These internal shifts create external results—businesses that reflect authentic purpose rather than market trends.

When you know why you are here, you stop living like you are lost. This clarity transforms decision-making across every aspect of business—from strategic planning to daily operations. Alignment between purpose and activity creates natural momentum that reduces friction and increases effectiveness. Missionpreneurs operate from this centered place, building enterprises that advance their calling rather than distracting from it.

The practical implementation of calling-driven business requires intentional alignment between purpose and operations. Every business decision becomes an opportunity to express calling or contradict it. By consistently choosing alignment, we build enterprises that feel like extensions of our purpose rather than obligations competing with it. This integration creates sustainable business models that energize rather than exhaust their founders.

Reflection Questions

1. Where in my life am I chasing validation instead of fulfilling assignment? How might this misalignment be affecting my business decisions and long-term sustainability?

2. What responsibilities feel internal—things I would feel wrong neglecting? How could these internal commitments inform my business model and strategic priorities?

3. What pressures might be confirming calling rather than exposing weakness? How can I reframe business

challenges as opportunities to express purpose rather than obstacles to overcome?

4. Where do I feel misaligned, and what is that misalignment costing me? What specific business activities drain my energy because they conflict with my calling?

5. If applause disappeared, what mission would I still commit to pursuing? How can I structure my business to advance this mission regardless of external validation?

Closing Declaration

I refuse to chase what was never assigned to me.

I release the need for applause, comparison, and validation.

I choose calling over convenience and alignment over adrenaline.

I will build my life on purpose, not pressure.

My effort will be anchored in identity, not emotion.

I am not running for attention.

I am fulfilling assignment.

I am a Missionpreneur. I stop chasing—and I start calling.

Chapter 4

Purpose: The Ultimate Performance Advantage

Why Purpose Beats Motivation, Hype, and Talent Every Time

Motivation is loud.

Purpose is quiet.

Motivation is emotional.

Purpose is foundational.

Motivation comes and goes.

Purpose remains when everything else fades.

Every athlete, entrepreneur, leader, coach, and competitor experiences days when they don't feel like showing up. The separating line between average and elite is not talent, opportunity, or even discipline—it is what drives them when feelings fail. This distinction becomes most evident during periods of challenge, when external rewards diminish and internal conviction must carry the weight of continued action. Those who achieve sustainable success have discovered that purpose provides the enduring fuel that motivation simply cannot supply.

When people are driven by emotion, consistency depends on convenience. When people are driven by purpose, consistency endures even when life is inconvenient. Purpose is not inspirational fluff; it is a biological and psychological anchor. When a person is aligned with what they were created to do, performance stabilizes at the deepest levels. Stress responses regulate. Decision-making sharpens. Confidence strengthens. Emotional resilience increases. Research consistently demonstrates that purpose-driven individuals maintain higher levels of performance during periods of uncertainty and recover more quickly from setbacks.

Purpose is not merely something you think.

Purpose is something you become anchored to.

The Day Hype Dies

Anyone can perform when life is exciting—when the crowd is cheering, momentum is easy, results come quickly, and attention is abundant. But hype always fades. Applause moves on. Attention shifts. Excitement eventually runs out. This pattern repeats in every business venture, creative project, and personal endeavor, creating a predictable valley where commitment is tested and true character emerges.

That is the moment where paths diverge. Average performers slow down or quit. Elite performers lock in. The divergence isn't subtle—it becomes the defining characteristic that separates those who create lasting impact from those who merely participate temporarily. Purpose-driven entrepreneurs continue building during economic downturns. Purpose-driven creators continue producing when trends shift. Purpose-driven leaders continue serving when recognition diminishes.

The defining question becomes simple and unavoidable: What drives you when nothing around you is driving you? If you require hype to function, you will not last long. But if you are fueled by purpose, endurance becomes inevitable. This principle applies whether leading a multinational organization or launching a solo venture—the sustainability of your effort directly correlates to the depth of your purpose.

Purpose outlives momentum. It sustains effort long after excitement disappears. It transforms the question from "Do I feel like continuing?" to "Does this matter enough to continue regardless of how I feel?"

Purpose and the Willingness to Suffer Well

Purpose-driven individuals are willing to do work that motivation will never sustain. They train when no one is watching. They prepare for worst-case scenarios. They rehearse adversity rather than hoping it never arrives. Purpose creates a tolerance—and even an appreciation—for discomfort when discomfort serves growth. This willingness to embrace necessary difficulty becomes a competitive advantage in markets where most participants seek only comfort and convenience.

This is why purpose-driven performers outlast more talented but less anchored peers. Talent may get attention early, but purpose keeps people consistent over decades. The business landscape is littered with once-promising ventures that collapsed not from lack of opportunity but from lack of purpose sufficient to weather inevitable challenges. Conversely, many industry leaders attribute their longevity not to superior resources but to unwavering commitment to their core mission.

Purpose is not about applause.

It is about alignment.

Biblical Example: Esther and the Courage of Calling

Esther's story reveals the true cost and power of purpose. She did not seek influence or spotlight. In fact, stepping into her assignment placed her life at risk. Yet the defining moment arrived when she was reminded that her position was not accidental: "Perhaps you were born for such a time as this." This perspective transformed her understanding from merely occupying a position to fulfilling a divine appointment—a shift that fundamentally altered her willingness to take necessary risks.

Purpose did not promise Esther safety. It demanded courage. It called her beyond preference and comfort into responsibility. Purpose reframed fear—not as something to avoid, but as confirmation that the assignment mattered. When facing potential death, her response—"If I perish, I perish"—demonstrates the prioritization that purpose creates: the mission becomes more important than personal comfort or even survival.

Biblical purpose does not eliminate risk. It provides meaning strong enough to overcome it. And meaning gives people the strength to do what fear would normally prevent. This principle applies directly to entrepreneurial ventures where risk is inevitable and courage becomes a prerequisite for meaningful impact. Purpose transforms risk assessment from "Is this safe?" to "Is this necessary for the mission?"

Purpose Unlocks Discipline

Discipline is not primarily a willpower issue; it is an alignment issue. When motivation is the driver, effort becomes inconsistent. People show up when they feel like it, commit when excitement is high, and disengage when resistance appears. This pattern creates the erratic performance that undermines long-term success in any meaningful endeavor, whether building a business, developing a skill, or leading an organization.

Purpose changes that equation. When you are aligned with your calling, discipline becomes identity. You show up because it is who you are. You train because it is non-negotiable. You commit not because it feels good, but because the mission matters more than the mood. This identity-based approach to discipline creates consistency that compounds over time, while motivation-based discipline constantly requires renewal.

Purpose turns discipline from a daily battle into a steady flow. It shifts the internal narrative from "I have to do this" to "I get to do this" and ultimately to "I am this." The most successful entrepreneurs, leaders, and innovators don't rely on discipline as an external force but experience it as the natural expression of purpose alignment.

Purpose Makes Pain Productive

Pain without purpose cripples. Pain with purpose develops. This distinction fundamentally alters how we experience difficulty and determines whether challenges strengthen or weaken our resolve. Purpose transforms the interpretation of pain from punishment to preparation, from obstacle to opportunity, from setback to setup.

Every meaningful pursuit involves discomfort—training, study, sacrifice, loss, disappointment, and delay. Without purpose, these experiences feel pointless and overwhelming. With purpose, they become refining forces. Market challenges become clarifying rather than discouraging. Competitive pressures become strengthening rather than threatening. Internal struggles become developmental rather than destructive.

Purpose does not remove difficulty. It gives difficulty meaning. Setbacks no longer signal failure; they signal formation. Pain becomes part of the process rather than proof of inadequacy. This perspective enables resilience that carries through inevitable valleys and creates the capacity to persist when others retreat. For the Missionpreneur, this means viewing business challenges not as evidence to quit but as invitations to grow.

Purpose Fixes Confidence at the Root

Most people try to build confidence through unstable sources—compliments, accomplishments, comparison, appearance, approval. Each of those fluctuates. Purpose-based confidence is different. It rests on alignment rather than perfection. This distinction creates psychological stability that withstands both criticism and praise, maintaining equilibrium regardless of external feedback.

Purpose-driven confidence says, I am here for a reason. This assignment belongs to me. Pressure cannot take what it did not give. This internal anchor provides the security necessary to take risks, make difficult decisions, and persist through uncertainty. Rather than deriving worth from outcomes, purpose-anchored individuals derive worth from alignment with their calling.

When confidence flows from purpose instead of performance, pressure loses its power to intimidate. Competitors become less threatening. Criticism becomes less destabilizing. Failure becomes less defining. This creates the psychological safety necessary for innovation, bold decision-making, and authentic leadership—all essential elements for entrepreneurial success and meaningful impact.

Discovering Purpose Through Movement

Purpose rarely arrives fully formed. Many people remain stuck because they expect clarity before action. In reality, purpose unfolds through movement. Curiosity sparks interest. Consistency builds rhythm. Conviction eventually forms—not because the path is easy, but because it becomes unmistakably yours. This progressive revelation means that waiting for complete clarity before beginning often becomes a permanent barrier to discovering your purpose.

For the Missionpreneur, this principle means starting with available clarity rather than waiting for complete certainty. It means taking action on current understanding while remaining open to refinement. It means treating purpose as an unfolding journey rather than a single moment of revelation. Each step of obedience reveals the next step, each commitment creates greater clarity, and each decision builds momentum toward fuller purpose alignment.

Purpose is not discovered through endless contemplation. It is revealed through faithful action over time. This practical approach to purpose discovery eliminates the paralysis of analysis and creates momentum that eventually clarifies calling. The most successful purpose-driven leaders didn't wait to start until they had perfect clarity—they gained clarity by starting and remaining faithful to what they understood at each stage.

Purpose Will Challenge Your Preferences

Purpose often leads people into responsibilities their preferences would never choose. Comfort seeks ease. Purpose pursues growth. Preference favors convenience. Purpose prioritizes impact. This inherent tension means that purpose fulfillment frequently requires embracing necessary discomfort rather than avoiding it. The path of greatest purpose rarely aligns with the path of least resistance.

For the Missionpreneur, this means recognizing that fulfilling your calling will regularly require decisions that contradict personal preference. It might mean having difficult conversations when you prefer harmony. It might mean embracing financial risk when you prefer security. It might mean developing new skills when you prefer operating within established competencies. Purpose consistently expands capacity by pushing beyond preference.

Comfort and calling rarely coexist. Growth demands tension. Purpose values meaning over momentary relief. This understanding transforms how we interpret discomfort—not as evidence we're on the wrong path, but often as confirmation we're embracing necessary growth. The most impactful leaders consistently choose purpose over preference, mission over comfort, and growth over convenience.

Purpose Is Stronger Than Circumstances

People without purpose feel limited by conditions. People with purpose assume responsibility despite conditions. Purpose is not fragile. It does not require perfect timing or ideal environments. It transforms adversity into opportunity. This resilience means purpose-driven individuals and organizations maintain momentum through challenges that derail others, converting obstacles into distinctive advantages.

The Missionpreneur approaches market challenges, resource limitations, and competitive pressures not as excuses for underperformance but as invitations to innovative problem-solving. Where others see barriers, the purpose-driven leader sees opportunities for differentiation. Where others retreat during difficulty, the purpose-anchored entrepreneur advances. This approach converts limitations from restrictive boundaries to creative catalysts.

Lives built on hype break easily. Lives built on purpose become unbreakable. Organizations driven by trends collapse under pressure. Organizations driven by purpose withstand market volatility. Ventures founded on convenience dissolve when challenged. Ventures founded on conviction endure through adversity. Purpose creates sustainability that transcends circumstances and builds legacy that outlasts trends.

Reflection Questions

1. Where in my life have emotions been driving decisions more than purpose? What specific choices would change if purpose became my primary decision filter?

2. What work would I continue even if recognition or reward disappeared? How can I structure more of my business activities around these intrinsically meaningful areas?

3. Where does my purpose need to become non-negotiable? What boundaries need strengthening to protect my core mission from dilution?

4. What past pain could become productive if connected to purpose? How might previous challenges provide unique perspective or capability for my current mission?

5. What decisions would change if I prioritized calling over comfort? Which current commitments exist primarily for convenience rather than conviction?

Closing Declaration

I do not rely on hype to sustain me.

I am anchored by purpose.

I choose meaning over momentum and calling over convenience.

Discipline flows from who I am, not how I feel.

Pressure refines me because purpose grounds me.

Pain develops me because purpose defines me.

I am aligned.

I am consistent.

I am unshakeable.

I am a Missionpreneur, and purpose is my advantage.

CHAPTER 5

FROM VISION TO INHERITANCE

Vision is powerful. But vision alone is fragile. Without proper implementation and structure, even the most compelling vision remains vulnerable to misinterpretation, dilution, and eventual dissolution.

Many leaders receive vision. Few convert vision into inheritance. Vision lives inside a person; inheritance lives inside a system. If what God revealed to you cannot be passed on, protected, and multiplied, it remains inspirational—but never becomes transformational. The transition from personal insight to organizational DNA requires intentional design and persistent implementation.

Vision may ignite the future, but inheritance secures it. Without inheritance, even the strongest vision eventually fades when the visionary steps away. True legacy emerges not from momentary inspiration but from sustainable implementation that transcends individual leadership.

The Limit of Vision

Vision is often celebrated as the pinnacle of leadership. We quote visionaries, attend vision-casting conferences, and admire bold foresight. Yet Scripture makes something unmistakably clear: vision was never meant to end with the one who received it. The divine design for vision always includes multiplication and continuation beyond its original recipient.

Moses saw the Promised Land, but Joshua led the people into it. David envisioned the temple, but Solomon built it. Vision initiates; inheritance completes. These biblical patterns reveal God's intention for vision to be transferred, not merely proclaimed. Each visionary served as a crucial link in a generational chain rather than the final destination.

A leader who clings too tightly to vision eventually becomes a bottleneck to the very future they were called to release. Vision that cannot move beyond its originator remains incomplete. When we grasp too firmly what was meant to flow through us, we inadvertently restrict its impact and limit its fulfillment.

Why Vision Often Dies with the Leader

Vision dies when it stays undocumented, untrained, unshared, and unprotected. Many leaders assume others naturally see what they see. They forget that vision is intuitive to the visionary but instructional to everyone else. This fundamental disconnect explains why countless organizations lose their direction after leadership transitions.

What feels obvious to you must be taught intentionally to others. If vision is not explained, practiced, and reinforced, it will be misunderstood or reshaped. Vision untaught does not multiply—it distorts. Each subsequent interpretation moves further from the original revelation until the essence is lost entirely.

The failure to translate personal conviction into organizational culture creates a dangerous dependency on the founder's presence. Without systematic transfer, vision remains personality-dependent rather than purpose-driven, creating an unsustainable model that cannot survive leadership transitions.

Vision Versus Inheritance

Vision declares direction. Inheritance governs behavior. While vision points toward possibility, inheritance establishes the pathways to reach it and sustain it. This distinction separates temporary initiatives from lasting legacies.

Vision energizes a moment. Inheritance sustains a culture. Vision is often carried by passion; inheritance is preserved through structure. Without inheritance, each generation must rebuild what the previous one already learned instead of advancing it further. This cyclical pattern prevents true progress and exhausts resources in perpetual reinvention.

Inheritance ensures continuity when personalities change, leadership transitions occur, and circumstances shift. It provides the framework through which vision can adapt to new challenges without abandoning core principles. While vision inspires commitment, inheritance creates consistency that transcends individual leadership seasons.

When Vision Quietly Becomes Ego

This is where vision can become dangerous. Some leaders do not actually desire inheritance—they desire admiration. They enjoy being the sole interpreter of vision. They unconsciously maintain dependency and equate control with care. This subtle shift from stewardship to ownership undermines the very purpose of the vision they received.

But biblical leadership is never about becoming irreplaceable. It is about making yourself unnecessary over time. Vision hoarded turns into pride. Vision released becomes legacy. The truest test of leadership is not what happens while you lead but what continues after you step aside.

Authentic visionaries measure their success not by personal recognition but by organizational reproduction. They find fulfillment in seeing others carry forward what they began, even when those successors receive the acclaim. This selfless perspective distinguishes genuine stewards from those seeking personal platforms.

Biblical Example: Moses, Joshua, and the Transfer of Authority

Moses stands as one of Scripture's clearest examples of vision received and responsibility transferred. Though he was used powerfully, Moses understood that the promise would not be fulfilled through him alone. Rather than resisting succession, he prepared Joshua publicly and intentionally, demonstrating the divine pattern for leadership transition.

Joshua was not simply informed; he was observed, corrected, commissioned, and empowered. Moses modeled obedience to God even when it meant releasing control. That transfer ensured continuity of mission rather than collapse after leadership change. Their relationship exemplifies how vision becomes inheritance through deliberate mentorship and gradual responsibility transfer.

Legacy leadership requires the humility to prepare others to finish what you will not. Moses' willingness to invest in Joshua despite knowing he himself would not enter the Promised Land reveals the selfless nature of true vision-carriers. His example challenges modern leaders to consider whether they are building organizations dependent on their presence or capable of thriving beyond their tenure.

The Missionpreneur Responsibility

Missionpreneurs refuse to let vision die with them. They take responsibility for translating revelation into structure. They ask what must be written, what must be modeled, and what must be multiplied. This proactive approach transforms abstract concepts into tangible systems that can be transferred to future stewards.

They understand the danger of imbalance. Vision without ownership creates confusion. Ownership without values creates drift. Values without systems create inconsistency. Missionpreneurs intentionally convert vision into inheritance pathways that outlive their leadership tenure. This comprehensive approach addresses both the philosophical foundation and practical implementation necessary for sustainable impact.

By integrating spiritual insight with organizational discipline, missionpreneurs build enterprises that maintain mission integrity across generations. They recognize that longevity requires both divine inspiration and human administration, refusing to sacrifice either in pursuit of lasting impact.

From Revelation to System

Vision becomes inheritance only when it descends into structure. Revelation must eventually inform mission, shape values, establish standards, and flow into systems. Legacy does not live in inspiration; it lives in processes that guide decisions long after the visionary is absent. This progression from concept to culture requires intentional design rather than organic evolution.

If vision never reaches the system level, it remains dependent on personality rather than protected by design. Systems create consistency that transcends individual interpretation, ensuring that core principles remain intact despite changing leadership styles. They transform subjective insights into objective frameworks that can be taught, measured, and reproduced.

The journey from revelation to system requires patience and persistence. What begins as spiritual insight must be translated into organizational language without losing its essence. This delicate balance preserves both the divine origin and practical application of the vision, making it both spiritually authentic and operationally viable.

The Unseen Work of Codification

Codifying vision is unglamorous but essential. It requires slowing down to write what feels intuitive, explaining what seems obvious, and repeating what feels redundant. Yet codification protects vision from drift, creates generational clarity, and removes personality dependence. This behind-the-scenes work rarely receives recognition but fundamentally determines longevity.

What is not written will not be remembered accurately. What is not clarified will be assumed—and assumption is the enemy of inheritance. Documentation creates a reference point that transcends memory and interpretation, establishing an authoritative source that future leaders can consult when questions arise.

Effective codification requires both precision and accessibility. It must capture nuance without creating complexity, providing clear guidance without restricting appropriate adaptation. This balance ensures the vision remains both protected and practical as it transfers from one generation to the next.

A Warning About Familiarity

The environments most vulnerable to drift are those marked by familiarity. Families, ministries, and organizations often assume shared understanding. Over time, assumptions replace alignment. What began as clear conviction gradually blurs through unspoken interpretations and unexplored differences in perspective.

Clarity may feel repetitive to a leader, but it feels stabilizing to the next generation. Inheritance thrives on explicit communication, not implied expectations. Regular reinforcement of foundational principles prevents the subtle erosion that occurs when values are assumed rather than articulated.

Familiarity creates a dangerous illusion of alignment without verifying its existence. Leaders must regularly assess whether shared language reflects shared understanding, creating forums for questions and clarification that prevent divergent interpretations from developing undetected.

Turning Values into Governance

Values only matter when they guide decisions. If values do not influence hiring, discipline, promotion, and accountability, they are decoration rather than direction. True organizational values manifest in consistent patterns of behavior rather than aspirational statements on office walls.

Inheritance requires governance—clear frameworks that protect future leaders from improvising the mission. Governance does not limit vision; it safeguards it. Well-designed governance structures provide both boundaries and flexibility, ensuring core principles remain intact while allowing appropriate adaptation to changing circumstances.

Effective governance balances principle with practicality, creating systems that reflect values without becoming rigid or bureaucratic. It establishes decision-making frameworks that guide rather than dictate, empowering future leaders to apply timeless principles to contemporary challenges without compromising essential convictions.

From Information to Impartation

Inheritance is not a document; it is a discipleship process. It grows through observation, participation, correction, and eventual ownership. Jesus did not simply explain the Kingdom—He modeled it and then entrusted others with responsibility. His pattern of "come and see" before "go and do" demonstrates the experiential nature of true inheritance.

True inheritance develops through apprenticeship, not lectures. Information transfer provides knowledge, but impartation creates capability. This distinction explains why many organizations possess extensive documentation but struggle with consistent implementation—they have shared information without developing capacity.

The discipleship model requires leaders to invest time in developing people rather than merely perfecting processes. This relational investment creates carriers of culture rather than merely followers of protocol, ensuring the spirit of the vision transfers alongside its structure.

The Inheritance Question

Here is the defining test: If I stepped away today, what would continue intact, and what would disappear with me? This penetrating question reveals the true state of your leadership legacy and organizational health. It distinguishes between what you've built and what you've merely maintained.

Anything that vanishes when you are gone was never inherited—it was merely carried. True inheritance continues without your presence because it has been fully transferred rather than temporarily delegated. This distinction separates sustainable impact from temporary influence.

Answering this question honestly requires both courage and humility. It may reveal uncomfortable gaps between intention and implementation, highlighting areas where dependency remains despite desires for durability. Yet this awareness creates the opportunity for intentional transition from vision-carrier to legacy-builder.

Reflection Questions

1. What aspects of the vision exist only in my head and not in writing or structure? Which key insights or principles remain undocumented or uncommunicated to my team?

2. Where have I confused control with stewardship? In what areas am I reluctant to delegate authority despite having capable people ready to assume responsibility?

3. What values need to be translated into clear standards or systems? Which principles are frequently mentioned but inconsistently practiced due to lack of structure?

4. Who am I intentionally developing to carry vision beyond my involvement? Have I identified and invested in specific individuals who demonstrate both capability and character alignment?

5. What parts of the mission would struggle if I stepped away tomorrow? Which processes or relationships remain dependent on my personal involvement rather than organizational systems?

Closing Declaration

I was not given vision to carry alone.

I was entrusted with vision so I could release it responsibly.

I commit to stewardship over control.

I will build systems that protect purpose beyond personality.

I will prepare successors rather than preserve dependence.

What God revealed to me will outlive me.

Vision entrusted to me is a gift.

Vision transferred through me becomes inheritance.

I am a Missionpreneur, and I build for generations.

CHAPTER 6

WHY MOST LEADERS NEVER
MULTIPLY

Most leadership problems are not skill problems. They are identity problems. The distinction is critical for any missionpreneur seeking sustainable impact rather than temporary influence.

Leaders stall not because they lack vision, effort, or intelligence, but because something deeper resists release. Multiplication requires more than competence. It requires trust, humility, and intentional surrender. That is the point where many leaders quietly stop—not publicly, but internally. This invisible threshold separates conventional leadership from transformational legacy.

They keep building. They keep leading. They keep working harder. But they stop multiplying. The symptoms appear gradually—increasing exhaustion, diminishing returns, and a nagging sense that growth has plateaued despite increased effort.

The Invisible Ceiling

Every leader eventually becomes the ceiling of their organization, family, or movement. Not because they are ineffective, but because they are indispensable. When everything flows through one person, decisions slow, innovation stalls, and the next generation waits for permission rather than developing initiative. This centralization creates a bottleneck that no amount of personal capacity can overcome.

What initially feels like strength slowly becomes strain. If growth depends on you, it will ultimately be limited by you. Multiplication cannot occur where dependence remains the primary operating system. The very strengths that built the organization become its greatest limitations when not transferred to others.

For missionpreneurs, this ceiling represents not just a leadership challenge but a fundamental threat to the mission itself. When impact can't extend beyond personal capacity, vision remains perpetually unrealized.

Control Disguised as Care

Most leaders don't intend to limit others. Control rarely announces itself honestly. It often wears the disguise of responsibility. I just want it done right. I'm protecting the mission. They're not ready yet. These justifications sound noble but function as barriers to development.

But prolonged hesitation often reveals something deeper—fear of being replaced, fear of losing relevance, or fear that others will expose weaknesses the leader has learned to manage privately.

Control may feel responsible, but it quietly starves multiplication. The leader's intentions may be protective, but the impact remains restrictive.

Care that never releases is not stewardship; it is insecurity. True care develops capability rather than dependency. It accepts short-term imperfection for long-term growth. It prioritizes development over perfection.

The Cost of Centralization

Centralized leadership creates early momentum but long-term fragility. When authority, knowledge, and decision-making remain concentrated, leaders burn out, teams disengage, families fracture, and organizations collapse during transition. The symptoms appear first as subtle inefficiencies, then as mounting frustration, and finally as structural failure.

Missionpreneurs understand a principle many leaders learn too late: what you refuse to decentralize, you eventually destroy. Multiplication requires distributed authority—not reckless freedom, but trained trust rooted in shared values. This distribution isn't abdication but strategic empowerment.

The organizational cost manifests in three dimensions: diminished innovation as diverse perspectives remain unheard, decreased engagement as capable people feel underutilized, and dangerous succession gaps as potential leaders remain undeveloped. What appears efficient in the short term becomes existentially threatening in the long term.

The Ego Trap

Ego does not always look loud or arrogant. Sometimes it appears subtle—being the only one "in the know," needing final approval on everything, or designing systems that quietly require your constant involvement. These patterns create an organizational architecture that reinforces dependency while appearing collaborative.

Ego resists multiplication because multiplication shifts attention away from the builder. But in God's economy, leadership is measured not by retention of control, but by release of capacity. True impact is measured not by what happens when you're present, but by what continues when you're absent.

For the missionpreneur, this requires regular self-examination. Are systems designed for control or multiplication? Do structures concentrate or distribute authority? Does success require your constant presence or can it flourish without you? The answers reveal whether ego or mission drives the enterprise.

Biblical Example: Jesus and the Risk of Release

Jesus provides the clearest model of true multiplication. He could have centralized authority, built a massive structure, and retained control. Instead, He chose a slower, riskier path that prioritized sustainable impact over immediate efficiency.

He trained twelve. He empowered seventy-two. He entrusted imperfect people with a perfect mission. And then He left. This deliberate strategy prioritized multiplication over management, development over dependency, and movement over monument.

Jesus did not establish a monument dependent on His presence; He launched a movement sustained by multiplication. He accepted the risk of failure because the greater risk was containment. Refusal to multiply would have ensured extinction. His investment in developing leaders rather than merely directing followers created exponential rather than linear impact.

Multiplication always involves risk. But refusing to multiply guarantees limitation. Every missionpreneur faces this fundamental choice between the security of control and the potential of multiplication.

From Delegation to Discipleship

Delegation distributes tasks. Discipleship transfers thinking, values, and judgment. Many leaders delegate work while withholding authority. They share labor but never share leadership. This creates efficiency without development—a temporary solution that prevents permanent transformation.

True multiplication follows a progression: explanation of why decisions are made, exposure to how leaders think, empowerment to decide independently, and evaluation that refines judgment. Leaders who are never trusted to decide are never trained to lead. The development process must include both instruction and implementation.

For missionpreneurs, this means creating intentional pathways for leadership development. It requires transparent decision-making, regular mentoring conversations, graduated authority, and consistent feedback loops. Without this structured approach, multiplication remains an aspiration rather than an achievement.

Diagnosing the Bottleneck

Every leader should periodically confront uncomfortable questions. How many decisions truly require my involvement? Who could decide this with proper training? What would break if I stepped away for thirty days? Who is being prepared to replace me—or portions of my role? These diagnostic questions reveal whether systems are designed for multiplication or dependency.

If the honest answer is no one, multiplication has already stalled. The bottleneck isn't in the organization's processes but in the leader's perspective. Addressing this requires both structural changes and personal transformation—systems that distribute authority and a mindset that celebrates release.

For family businesses and legacy-focused enterprises, this diagnosis is particularly crucial. The transition between generations often fails not because successors lack ability, but because predecessors never truly transferred authority, knowledge, and relationships. Multiplication must be intentional long before transition becomes necessary.

Failure, Fragmentation, and Formation

Leaders often fear that releasing authority will lead to mistakes. Mistakes, however, refine leaders. Silence stagnates them. The greater danger is fragmentation—distributed authority without shared values. This creates inconsistency, confusion, and eventual conflict as different leaders pursue divergent priorities.

That is why multiplication must be anchored in clearly articulated values, documented decision standards, and consistent accountability. Freedom without formation destroys. Formation without freedom suffocates. Effective multiplication requires both clear boundaries and genuine authority.

For missionpreneurs, this balance is achieved through intentional culture-building. Values must be explicitly identified, consistently reinforced, and practically applied. Decision frameworks should provide guidance without micromanagement. Accountability systems should measure outcomes rather than activities. This creates alignment without uniformity.

The Missionpreneur Pathway to Multiplication

Missionpreneurs build leadership pipelines rather than dependency chains. People first observe leadership in action. Then they participate alongside it. Eventually they are entrusted with authority. True legacy begins when those leaders train others in turn. This four-stage process transforms individual leadership into organizational multiplication.

Anything short of that final stage is leadership—but it is not multiplication. Many organizations develop capable leaders but never create multiplicative systems. The distinction is critical: leadership development creates capable individuals; multiplication creates self-sustaining systems that generate leaders continuously.

For mission-driven enterprises, this pathway must be intentionally designed, consistently implemented, and regularly evaluated. It requires identifying potential leaders early, providing graduated responsibility, offering regular feedback, and celebrating successful transition. The process should be documented, communicated, and refined over time.

Why Multiplication Feels Like Loss

Multiplication requires leaders to grieve their own centrality. It feels like losing importance, sharing credit, and allowing others to improve upon what you started. Healthy legacy demands choosing impact over identity. This emotional transition is often more challenging than the operational handover.

If leadership becomes your identity, you will resist multiplication. If obedience becomes your identity, you will pursue it. Missionpreneurs understand that the mission is always bigger than the messenger. This perspective shift requires regular self-examination and intentional identity formation anchored in purpose rather than position.

The emotional journey includes recognizing when your presence limits growth, celebrating others' success even when it eclipses your own, finding fulfillment in development rather than direction, and discovering new avenues for contribution as others assume previous responsibilities. This transition from builder to multiplier represents the highest form of leadership maturity.

The Multiplication Metric

The clearest test of multiplication is simple: Who can lead effectively without you—and who are they training? If leadership stops with you, the mission stops with you. This metric measures not just current capacity but future sustainability. It reveals whether you're building a dependent organization or a multiplicative movement.

For missionpreneurs, this metric should be regularly assessed, honestly evaluated, and strategically addressed. It requires identifying leadership gaps, creating development opportunities, gradually transferring authority, and celebrating successful multiplication. The goal isn't just capable leaders but leaders who develop other leaders.

True multiplication creates geometric rather than arithmetic growth. Each leader developed becomes a source of additional leadership development. The impact extends exponentially beyond the founder's direct influence, creating sustainability that outlasts any individual contribution.

Reflection Questions

1. Where am I unintentionally creating dependency rather than development? What systems or habits reinforce this pattern?
2. What fears surface when I consider releasing authority? What underlying beliefs drive these concerns?
3. Which decisions could be trained rather than retained? What frameworks would enable others to make these decisions effectively?
4. Who am I actively discipling to think, decide, and lead? What intentional process am I using for their development?
5. What would need to change for multiplication to accelerate? What personal or organizational barriers must be addressed?
6. How would our mission advance if multiplication became our primary leadership metric? What new possibilities would emerge?

7. Where have I confused care with control? How might releasing authority actually serve others better than retaining it?

Closing Declaration

I was not called to carry everything.

I was called to multiply leaders.

I choose release over control and trust over fear.

I will develop people, not dependency.

I will build pipelines, not bottlenecks.

My impact will extend beyond my involvement.

I will measure success not by what I accomplish but by what I enable.

I will find fulfillment in others' growth, not just my own achievements.

I will create systems that multiply leadership, not just manage tasks.

Control builds empires.

Multiplication builds movements.

I am a Missionpreneur, and I lead to release—not to retain.

CHAPTER 7

ALIGNMENT OVER ADRENALINE

Building Performance That Lasts After the Hype Dies

Adrenaline can start a race.

Only alignment can finish it.

Anyone can be great for a moment.

Only the aligned remain great for a lifetime.

Adrenaline is emotional. Alignment is structural. Adrenaline produces explosive bursts of effort; alignment produces steady, unstoppable progress. The world rewards hype—big launches, dramatic beginnings, and loud declarations of motivation. But every beginning eventually fades into the mundane reality of daily execution. When the excitement disappears, the truth emerges about what truly drives sustainable success in both business and life.

Were you driven by adrenaline, or guided by alignment?

Adrenaline burns fast and leaves you depleted. Alignment builds slowly but creates enduring momentum. Adrenaline depends on how you feel in the moment—vulnerable to external circumstances and internal moods. Alignment depends on who you are at your core—your values, mission, and identity. And when adversity arrives—as it inevitably does in every meaningful endeavor—adrenaline retreats while alignment grows stronger, providing the foundation for breakthrough when others falter.

The Adrenaline Trap

Adrenaline convinces you that you're ready for the grind—until the grind begins. Starting anything feels exciting at first. New seasons, new goals, new habits, new commitments all carry momentum. But excitement is temporary, often lasting only days or weeks before reality sets in. Calling is permanent—it sustains you through months and years of consistent effort. The adrenaline trap lures entrepreneurs into starting ventures they lack the alignment to sustain.

The moment hype evaporates, people discover what truly drives them. Those fueled by emotion stall when enthusiasm fades, abandoning projects when they no longer feel inspired. Those anchored in assignment continue regardless of emotional fluctuations, because alignment does not require excitement to operate. This distinction separates businesses that survive from those that thrive long-term.

Biblical Example: David Before Goliath

David's victory over Goliath is often framed as a moment of spontaneous courage, but Scripture reveals something deeper. David did not defeat the giant because of an emotional surge or temporary motivation. He prevailed because of alignment forged long before the moment arrived—alignment between his identity, skills, and divine purpose that created inevitable victory.

Years in obscurity shaped his identity and competence. Fighting lions and bears while protecting sheep, trusting God in isolation when no one witnessed his faithfulness, honing skill with a sling through thousands of repetitions, and showing up faithfully when unseen formed habits that could not be shaken. When David stepped onto the battlefield, he did not rise to the occasion through adrenaline—he revealed who he already was through alignment.

Alignment carried David into a moment adrenaline could never sustain. His victory wasn't emotional; it was structural—built on the foundation of who he had become through consistent, purpose-driven action.

Why Alignment Wins Psychologically

Adrenaline is short-term fuel. It spikes emotion, intensity, and aggression, but it crashes just as quickly, leaving a performance deficit and decision fatigue in its wake. Alignment is long-term fuel. It stabilizes identity, discipline, confidence, and precision under pressure, creating sustainable output regardless of circumstances. This psychological advantage becomes particularly evident during market downturns, competitive challenges, and unexpected obstacles.

Burnout does not come from hard work; it comes from misaligned work. People collapse when they depend on adrenaline, forcing themselves to perform activities disconnected from their purpose and values. Breakthrough happens when performance flows from purpose rather than emotion, creating a renewable energy source that grows stronger through use rather than depleting over time.

Identifying the Difference

When effort depends on excitement, validation, or visibility, adrenaline is in control. This manifests as inconsistent performance, emotional decision-making, and vulnerability to external opinions. But when people show up regardless of mood, protect standards without applause, and execute even on difficult days when motivation is absent, alignment is at work. The aligned entrepreneur maintains quality standards even when no one would notice a compromise.

Adrenaline fades when results slow, causing abandonment of initiatives at the first sign of difficulty. Alignment endures when adversity increases, viewing obstacles as confirmation of the path's importance rather than reasons to quit. One builds momentary momentum; the other builds sustainable mastery that compounds over time, creating competitive advantages that cannot be easily replicated.

Alignment Begins with Identity

Alignment is not about occasionally doing the right things. It is about becoming the right person consistently. Adrenaline asks what you feel like doing in the moment. Alignment asks what matches who you are and who you are becoming. This identity-based approach transforms decision-making from a constant struggle to a natural expression of character.

When identity is rooted in calling, behavior becomes predictable and consistent. Alignment is not about perfection; it is about reliability—showing up as the same person day after day. Consistency emerges naturally when actions flow from identity instead of emotion, creating trustworthiness that becomes the foundation of long-term business relationships and reputation.

The Quiet Advantage of Aligned Performers

Aligned performers conserve energy by avoiding five common drains: comparison that creates envy, entitlement that breeds disappointment, shortcuts that require rework, drama that wastes focus, and validation-seeking that surrenders control. They are anchored by responsibility, structure, purpose, and identity that generate internal motivation. They do not wait for emotional hype to begin the work. They respond to mission with immediate action regardless of circumstances.

That quiet consistency becomes a competitive advantage most people never develop. While competitors oscillate between hyperactivity and burnout, the aligned entrepreneur maintains steady progress, achieving in months what others fail to accomplish in years of inconsistent effort.

The Unseen Work That Builds Alignment

Alignment is forged in unglamorous moments—early mornings before the world awakens, late nights after others have quit, reviewing details others consider boring, mental training when physical training is easier, self-awareness practices that reveal uncomfortable truths, prayer that centers priorities, discipline that constrains impulses, and repeated failure followed by persistent recommitment. Adrenaline avoids that work. Alignment depends on it as the foundation for sustainable success.

Many confuse boredom with burnout. They are not the same. Burnout signals misalignment between values and activities. Boredom often signals that consistency is being trained—the necessary repetition that builds excellence. The aligned entrepreneur embraces necessary monotony, understanding that mastery requires thousands of unremarkable moments before producing remarkable results.

Alignment Simplifies Life

When you are aligned, confusion fades and clarity emerges. You don't negotiate with excuses or collapse when attention disappears. You don't need stimulation to stay committed to your path. Alignment replaces chaos with structure, eliminating the constant revaluation that drains decision-making energy from the misaligned. This simplification creates bandwidth for innovation where it matters most.

Adrenaline says, give me excitement.

Alignment says, give me systems.

Structure is how greatness becomes inevitable. The aligned entrepreneur creates frameworks, routines, and processes that ensure consistent execution regardless of emotional state. These systems transform aspirations into reality through the power of accumulated consistent action.

Building Alignment Intentionally

Alignment grows when calling is clarified through reflection and feedback, identity is defined through conscious choice rather than circumstance, routines are protected from interruption and compromise, and emotional negotiation is eliminated through pre-commitment. Progress is measured consistently against meaningful metrics, and environments are chosen wisely to support rather than undermine core values. People who live on adrenaline cannot sustain the pace of those building on alignment.

Alignment is not accidental. It is engineered through deliberate choices about how time is invested, which relationships are cultivated, what information is consumed, and which priorities receive focused attention. The aligned entrepreneur designs their business and life to naturally reinforce their most important values and objectives.

Why Alignment Makes You Dangerous

People driven by adrenaline can be outlasted. They burn bright but extinguish quickly when facing sustained resistance. People rooted in alignment are dangerous because they do not disappear after failure, lose identity after mistakes, or require permission to keep moving toward their objectives. They maintain momentum through setbacks that stop others completely. They do not chase destiny—they become someone destiny cannot ignore through the magnetic power of consistent purpose-driven action.

Alignment does not create loud lives.

It creates unstoppable ones.

Reflection Questions

1. Where in my life have I been fueled more by adrenaline than alignment? What has this cost me in terms of consistency and long-term results?
2. Which habits disappear when excitement fades? How could I redesign these to operate based on identity rather than emotion?
3. What structure would make my consistency automatic? What specific systems need implementation in my daily routine?
4. What identity statement could anchor my daily behavior when motivation fluctuates? How would I complete "I am someone who always..."?
5. What part of my calling needs to become non-negotiable now? Which aspect of my mission requires immediate protection from compromise?

Closing Declaration

I will not build my life on hype.

I choose alignment over adrenaline.

I am anchored in calling, not emotion.

I show up because it is who I am, not how I feel.

Structure protects my purpose.

Consistency reveals my identity.

When excitement fades, I remain.

When pressure rises, I advance.

I am not moment-driven—I am mission-anchored.

I am a Missionpreneur, and alignment makes me unstoppable.

CHAPTER 8

THE DARK SIDE OF AMBITION

When Success Becomes Toxic and Identity Gets Warped

Ambition is a gift—until it becomes a god. When properly channeled, ambition serves as the catalyst for extraordinary achievement and personal growth. However, when misaligned, it transforms into a destructive force that erodes our fundamental sense of self-worth and purpose.

In its purest form, ambition is a force for growth. It pushes you forward when others stay comfortable. It sharpens your focus, fuels discipline, wakes you up early, and keeps you up late. Ambition is the engine behind excellence, progress, and innovation. Many of the world's greatest achievements were built by people who refused to settle for mediocrity and instead pursued their vision with unwavering determination.

But ambition carries a shadow—a darker dimension that emerges when we lose perspective on its proper role in our lives.

This shadow doesn't announce itself dramatically; rather, it creeps in gradually, reshaping our relationship with success in subtle yet profound ways.

When ambition shifts from being fuel to being identity, something dangerous happens internally—often quietly, often unnoticed, until the damage is already done. You don't just want to succeed anymore. You need to succeed in order to feel valuable. Winning stops being a goal and becomes a requirement for self-worth. The stakes escalate from professional achievement to existential validation, creating an unsustainable psychological burden.

And when winning becomes the only way to feel worthy, success stops being meaningful and starts becoming toxic. The very achievements that should bring satisfaction instead create temporary relief followed by heightened anxiety about maintaining status or reaching the next milestone. This perpetual cycle of striving without fulfillment represents ambition at its most destructive.

There is nothing wrong with wanting more. Healthy desire for growth and achievement drives innovation, excellence, and positive transformation. There is something deeply disordered about needing more just to believe you matter. This distinction represents the crucial dividing line between ambition as empowerment and ambition as enslavement.

Success is beautiful when it is an expression of identity.

Success is destructive when it becomes the source of identity.

Ambition Was Never Meant to Carry Your Worth

Most people were never taught how to hold ambition correctly. Our cultural narratives celebrate hunger, grind, and hustle, but rarely teach restraint, alignment, or identity. We glorify the external manifestations of achievement while neglecting the internal foundations that give those achievements meaning and sustainability.

The result is a generation of high achievers who appear successful on the outside but are internally exhausted, anxious, and empty. They've climbed the ladder only to discover it was leaning against the wrong wall. Their accomplishments, impressive as they may be, fail to deliver the fulfillment they promised because they were pursued for the wrong reasons.

Ambition was never meant to tell you who you are. It was meant to help you steward who you already are. This fundamental reversal of order—allowing achievement to define identity rather than expressing it—creates a fragile foundation for both professional success and personal wellbeing. When your sense of self depends on external validation, you become vulnerable to every market fluctuation, criticism, or competitive threat.

When ambition becomes your identity, rest feels unsafe. Slowing down feels like falling behind. Saying no feels like losing relevance. You start chasing success not because you love the work, but because you are terrified of what it would mean to stop. Vacations trigger anxiety, weekends become work sessions, and relationships suffer as achievement becomes the singular priority. The joy of the journey evaporates, replaced by a desperate need to reach the next destination.

That is no longer ambition. That is addiction. And like all addictions, it demands increasing doses to produce diminishing returns, creating a spiral of striving that never reaches satisfaction.

Healthy Ambition vs. Unhealthy Ambition

There are two very different kinds of ambition, and they come from completely different places. Understanding the distinction is crucial for missionpreneurs who seek to create meaningful impact without sacrificing their wellbeing or integrity in the process.

Healthy ambition flows from purpose. It serves calling rather than ego. It aligns with identity rather than replacing it. It builds others along the way instead of leaving casualties. It endures even when applause disappears. This form of ambition is regenerative rather than depleting, creating energy through alignment with deeper values and mission.

Unhealthy ambition flows from insecurity. It serves ego. It attaches worth to outcomes. It competes destructively. It collapses when recognition fades. This form of ambition is ultimately unsustainable, creating a fragile success built on external validation rather than internal conviction. When the inevitable challenges arise, this foundation crumbles.

Healthy ambition says, I work hard because I'm called to.

Unhealthy ambition says, I work hard because I'm nothing without success.

One produces freedom—the liberty to pursue excellence without being defined by outcomes. The other produces slavery—often masked as achievement. This slavery manifests as constant anxiety, inability to enjoy success, competitive obsession, and loss of perspective about what truly matters.

Biblical Example: Saul and David—Two Ambitions, Two Trajectories

Scripture gives a striking contrast between two leaders who were both anointed, gifted, and capable—yet destroyed or elevated by the source of their ambition. Their parallel stories provide a powerful case study in how the foundation of ambition determines its ultimate outcome.

Saul was driven by approval. His identity was tied to how others saw him. When the crowd praised David more than him, Saul's insecurity was exposed. He became suspicious, reactive, jealous, and obsessed with preserving image rather than obeying God. His leadership deteriorated as his focus shifted from serving his calling to protecting his position. Eventually, his insecurity-driven decisions cost him not only his effectiveness but his kingdom.

David, on the other hand, was anchored in calling. He didn't need the spotlight to remain obedient. He didn't unravel when seasons were slow or invisible. He valued alignment over applause and obedience over image. Even during his years as a fugitive, hiding in caves while anointed as king, David maintained his integrity and purpose. His identity remained secure even when his circumstances were uncertain.

Saul chased validation and lost the crown.

David chased purpose and kept rising.

Talent can earn you success, but only identity determines whether success develops you—or destroys you. This principle applies directly to missionpreneurs who must navigate the complex interplay between ambition and purpose as they build ventures that matter.

How Ambition Quietly Turns Toxic

Unhealthy ambition rarely announces itself loudly. It doesn't arrive saying, I'm about to ruin your life. It often shows up as dedication, discipline, and drive—qualities we rightfully celebrate in business and leadership. The transformation happens gradually, through subtle shifts in motivation and mindset that eventually reshape our relationship with achievement.

You may be drifting into the dark side of ambition if rest makes you anxious, if you feel guilty when you're not producing, or if you constantly compare yourself to others even after winning. These warning signs indicate that ambition has crossed the line from motivation to identity. Other indicators include difficulty celebrating achievements before immediately focusing on the next goal, basing your mood entirely on recent performance, or feeling threatened rather than inspired by others' success.

Failure stops feeling like information and starts feeling like an indictment of who you are. Rather than viewing setbacks as valuable feedback that refines your approach, you experience them as personal deficiencies that threaten your worth. This perspective makes genuine risk-taking increasingly difficult, as the stakes have shifted from professional outcomes to personal value.

When success no longer feels fulfilling, it's not because success is broken. It's because the reason you're chasing it is broken. The achievements themselves aren't the problem—it's the expectation that they will provide what only a secure identity can deliver: a sense of inherent worth and purpose that transcends performance.

The Lie of "Not Enough Yet"

Unhealthy ambition runs on a dangerous narrative: not enough yet. This perpetual postponement of satisfaction creates a horizon that continually recedes, ensuring that fulfillment always remains just out of reach. The specific manifestations of this narrative vary, but the structure remains consistent.

When I get that job, then I'll feel secure.

When I make that money, then I'll relax.

When I win that title, then I'll finally feel confident.

When I reach that level, then I'll matter.

But every time you reach a milestone, the finish line moves. The goalposts shift, and suddenly the achievement that was supposed to bring contentment becomes merely a stepping stone to the next requirement. The satisfaction you expected never arrives, because success was never designed to carry your worth. No external achievement can fulfill what is fundamentally an internal need.

If success is where you get your identity, failure becomes a threat to your existence. That is when ambition becomes a prison. You're no longer running toward something—you're running from yourself. This desperate flight from inadequacy creates a relentless pace that eventually undermines both performance and wellbeing.

What Happens When This Isn't Healed

When ambition is driven by insecurity, it eventually produces predictable fruit: anxiety, burnout, jealousy, anger, isolation, obsession, and self-contempt. These consequences emerge not as random misfortunes but as the natural result of ambition that has lost its proper foundation. The manifestations may differ based on personality and circumstance, but the underlying pattern remains consistent.

The grind no longer energizes you—it defines you. What began as passionate pursuit becomes compulsive striving. You don't rest because you love the work; you refuse to rest because stopping feels like losing yourself. The very drive that once propelled you forward now prevents you from experiencing the satisfaction of arrival.

People don't destroy themselves because they stop caring. They destroy themselves because they care for the wrong reasons. This misplaced care creates a particularly dangerous form of self-destruction—one that masquerades as dedication and excellence while gradually eroding the foundation of sustainable success.

They are no longer pursuing excellence. They are trying to outrun emptiness. This distinction explains why many high achievers find themselves simultaneously successful and unsatisfied, accomplished yet anxious. The external achievements cannot fill the internal void they were never designed to address.

The Identity Reset: Healing the Dark Side of Ambition

The answer is not to abandon ambition. For missionpreneurs especially, ambition remains essential for creating meaningful impact and building ventures that matter. The answer is to purify it—to restore ambition to its proper role as the expression of identity rather than its source.

You don't need to stop wanting greatness. You need to stop needing greatness to feel valuable. Identity must come before ambition. Ambition must serve identity—not replace it. This reordering creates a foundation for sustainable success that doesn't consume the very person achieving it.

When ambition is purified, something powerful happens internally. Failure stops defining you. Criticism loses control. Pressure no longer dictates behavior. Values are no longer negotiable. Applause becomes optional. This internal freedom creates a paradoxical result: you often achieve more when achievement is no longer your primary source of worth.

Ambition becomes healthy when it grows out of purpose instead of insecurity. This transformation doesn't happen automatically or overnight. It requires intentional reflection, honest self-assessment, and often the support of mentors and community who can help restore perspective when it becomes distorted.

When Ambition Becomes Safe Again

Healthy ambition sounds different. It says, I want to win—not to prove who I am, but to express who I already am. This subtle but profound shift changes everything about how we pursue success and how we experience both achievement and setback. The reward is no longer attention. The reward is alignment.

Success becomes enjoyable again. When achievement no longer carries the burden of defining your worth, you can actually experience the satisfaction it naturally provides. Competition becomes energizing rather than consuming. Pressure becomes fuel instead of fear. You stop trying to impress the world and start fulfilling the assignment placed on your life.

That is ambition restored to its proper place. This restored ambition allows missionpreneurs to pursue bold visions without sacrificing their wellbeing or compromising their values in the process. It creates sustainable impact that flows from identity rather than consuming it.

Three Anchors That Keep Ambition Healthy

First, identity must be disconnected from performance. Performance should express your worth, not prove it. Until that belief is internalized, ambition will always carry unnecessary weight. This separation doesn't diminish the importance of excellence—it actually enhances it by allowing performance to flow from a secure foundation rather than a desperate need to establish value.

Second, success must be defined by alignment, not attention. Faithfulness to calling matters more than public recognition. If the world claps, remain anchored. If the world ignores you, remain anchored. This consistent orientation toward purpose rather than praise creates resilience through market fluctuations, criticism, and the inevitable seasons when recognition lags behind contribution.

Third, purpose must be protected from ego. Before major decisions, opportunities, or risks, leaders must ask a hard question: Am I serving calling, or am I feeding insecurity? When calling leads, you win. When insecurity leads, you lose—even if it looks like success. This regular self-assessment prevents the gradual drift from purpose-driven to ego-driven ambition that often occurs unconsciously.

Ambition at Its Highest Form

Ambition is only dangerous when ego is driving. But when purpose leads and character governs, ambition becomes inspiring, empowering, fulfilling, and sustainable. This purified ambition creates not just external achievements but internal alignment—a congruence between who you are and what you do that generates authentic satisfaction and impact.

You stop chasing success and start becoming someone success can't ignore. This transformation happens not through strategic positioning or personal branding, but through the magnetic authenticity that emerges when ambition flows from secure identity rather than attempting to create it. People are drawn to leaders whose ambition serves something greater than themselves.

That is ambition at its healthiest—and at its most dangerous, in the best possible way. It threatens status quo systems, challenges mediocrity, and refuses to settle for less than what's possible. As missionpreneurs, this form of ambition becomes our most powerful tool for creating ventures that matter and leaving a legacy that lasts.

Reflection Questions

1. Where has ambition drifted from purpose toward insecurity in my life? What specific areas of achievement have become overly connected to my sense of worth?

2. What part of success do I rely on to feel valuable? Is it recognition, financial outcomes, growth metrics, or something else?

3. How do I interpret failure—information for growth or indictment of identity? What was my internal response to my most recent significant setback?

4. Who would I be, and how would I live, if success disappeared for a season? What would remain if all external achievements were temporarily removed?

5. What belief about my identity would make ambition safe, enjoyable, and powerful again? What truth needs to be internalized to restore ambition to its proper role?

Closing Declaration

I reject ambition that demands success to prove my worth.

My value is established, not earned.

I choose purpose over pressure and alignment over approval.

I will pursue excellence without sacrificing integrity.

Ambition will serve my calling, not replace my identity.

I am free to win, free to fail, and free to grow.

Success does not define me.

Calling anchors me.

I am a Missionpreneur, and my ambition is healed, aligned, and powerful.

CHAPTER 9

PRESSURE IS A PRIVILEGE

What Performance Reveals—and Why It Never Lies

Pressure does not create weakness.

Pressure exposes weakness.

Pressure does not create strength.

Pressure reveals strength.

Pressure does not destroy identity.

Pressure reveals identity.

When moments get heavy—when eyes are watching, stakes are high, mistakes have consequences, and outcomes matter—the real you shows up. Not the rehearsed version. Not the highlight reel. Not the curated persona. Pressure strips away illusion and pulls truth to the surface, revealing the foundation you've built through consistent daily actions. This unveiling process happens in business negotiations, leadership challenges, family crises, and every domain where outcomes truly matter.

That is why most people fear pressure. They believe it can ruin them. In reality, pressure only reveals what has already been built—or neglected—inside them. The entrepreneur who crumbles during a critical pitch meeting isn't failing because of the pressure; they're experiencing the consequences of inadequate preparation, unclear vision, or misaligned values that existed long before the meeting began.

Pressure is not punishment.

Pressure is clarity.

Why Pressure Feels So Threatening

Pressure feels threatening because it removes excuses. When circumstances are calm, people can hide behind preparation gaps, emotional swings, and unfinished growth. Under pressure, none of that survives. Pressure shuts down pretending. The marketplace doesn't care about your intentions or what you meant to accomplish—it responds only to what you actually deliver when stakes are real.

This is why pressure is uncomfortable for people who rely on image instead of identity. Pressure doesn't ask who you want to be—it asks who you are. It strips away the comfort of potential and demands evidence of development. In business and leadership, this means the difference between those who talk about excellence and those who consistently produce it.

High-stakes moments don't change people. They expose them. The executive who micromanages during crisis isn't becoming controlling—they're revealing a lack of trust that was always present. The team that innovates during industry disruption isn't suddenly becoming creative—they're demonstrating a culture of adaptability they've intentionally cultivated.

The Lie of Talent and the Truth of Pressure

Our culture worships talent. Talent gets opportunities, scholarships, platforms, promotions, and praise. Talent is labeled "special" and treated as destiny. We celebrate the natural abilities, the quick studies, and the effortless achievers, often overlooking the more essential qualities that determine lasting success.

But pressure has no interest in talent. It dismisses potential in favor of performance. It ignores what you might do and focuses entirely on what you actually deliver when circumstances become demanding.

Pressure asks harder questions. Do you train when nobody is clapping? Do you believe when doubt is loud? Do you execute when consequences are real? Do you stay calm when chaos erupts? Do you lead when everything starts breaking? These questions separate those who merely possess capability from those who consistently convert capability into results.

If talent alone created greatness, elite performance would be common. Instead, pressure exposes a brutal truth: many people look like champions until the lights turn on. Markets are filled with businesses that appeared promising until customer demands intensified. Industries are littered with once-rising stars who faded when competition increased. Pressure brings honesty to every arena, revealing the gap between potential and performance.

Biblical Example: Peter on the Water—A Lesson in Pressure Psychology

The story of Peter walking on water reveals something profound about pressure. Peter did not sink because the storm intensified. The waves did not suddenly become stronger. The environment didn't change. The external conditions remained constant throughout his experience.

Peter sank because his focus shifted. His attention moved from the extraordinary possibility before him to the overwhelming circumstances around him. He moved from calling to consequence. From "I'm built for this" to "What if I fail?" The storm didn't defeat him. Self-doubt did. His internal dialogue changed, and his performance immediately followed.

This is the nature of pressure. Pressure itself is external. The collapse happens internally. Pressure is not the problem—your interpretation of pressure is. The same market conditions that bankrupt one company become the catalyst for another's innovation. The same industry challenges that paralyze one leader inspire creative solutions in another. The difference lies not in the pressure but in the response.

Why Most People Misread Pressure

Most people experience pressure as danger. Their internal dialogue sounds like this: I'm nervous. I might choke. This is too big. I can't mess this up. I don't want to be embarrassed. They interpret high-stakes moments as threats to their security, reputation, or self-image. This narrative transforms opportunity into anxiety.

That dialogue produces anxiety, hesitation, and self-protection—the enemy of execution. When self-preservation becomes the primary goal, innovation suffers, risk-taking diminishes, and performance becomes cautious rather than committed. The very qualities needed for breakthrough disappear precisely when they're most needed.

Elite performers interpret pressure differently. They don't say, This moment could expose me. They say, This moment will reveal me. They view pressure as confirmation of their readiness, not a threat to their adequacy. Market challenges become opportunities to demonstrate capability. Leadership tests become platforms for displaying character. Competitive pressure becomes the context for differentiation.

Pressure doesn't ask for perfection.

Pressure asks for alignment.

Pressure is not a threat—it is a mirror. It reflects back what you've built, what you value, what you believe, and what you prioritize. It shows where your systems work and where they break.

And mirrors are valuable, even when they are uncomfortable. They provide the feedback necessary for growth, the clarity required for improvement, and the honesty essential for transformation. What pressure reveals becomes the roadmap for development.

Three Pressure Responses—and What They Reveal

Under pressure, people consistently fall into one of three categories. These response patterns appear across industries, cultures, and contexts, revealing fundamental truths about how individuals navigate demanding circumstances.

Some collapse. Their internal script is fear-based. What if I fail? Their execution becomes tentative and inconsistent. Fear takes the wheel. They overthink decisions, second-guess instincts, and operate from worst-case scenarios. Their performance diminishes precisely when excellence is most needed. In business, these individuals make reactive decisions, abandon strategy during difficulty, and lose confidence when challenges intensify.

Some survive. Their script is ego-based. Just don't mess up. They play small, protect themselves, and do enough to avoid embarrassment. They survive pressure—but never dominate it. Their focus remains on maintaining image rather than maximizing impact. These professionals meet minimum expectations, avoid innovation during uncertainty, and prioritize safety over opportunity. They build businesses that survive but rarely scale, and careers that progress but seldom transform industries.

Some attack. Their script is identity-based. I'm built for this. They remain composed, confident, and decisive. They don't rush or freeze. They execute. Their focus stays on opportunity rather than threat, possibility rather than limitation. These individuals make their best decisions during crisis, find clarity amid confusion, and deliver their strongest performances when stakes are highest. They build resilient organizations, lead breakthrough initiatives, and consistently outperform during industry disruption.

All three may have talent.

Only one has assignment-level identity.

Talent collapses.

Ego survives.

Calling attacks.

That mindset is not instinct.

It is trained. It develops through intentional exposure to pressure, honest evaluation of performance, and consistent refinement of response patterns. The ability to perform under pressure becomes a competitive advantage that separates market leaders from participants.

From Fear to Activation: The Identity Shift

Pressure doesn't stop hurting until interpretation changes. The discomfort of high-stakes moments doesn't diminish through avoidance—it transforms through reframing. This mental shift represents one of the most significant competitive advantages available to entrepreneurs, leaders, and organizations.

Fear-driven thinking says, Pressure means I might fail.

Calling-driven thinking says, Pressure means I'm ready.

Fear says, I don't want to be exposed.

Calling says, This is where who I am becomes visible.

Champions don't wait for pressure to disappear. They train themselves to operate inside pressure. They develop systems, mindsets, and practices that function optimally when circumstances intensify. They create decision frameworks that remain accessible during complexity. They build teams capable of executing with precision regardless of external conditions.

Pressure becomes powerful when you stop resisting it and start respecting it. When you recognize pressure as validation rather than threat, the entire experience transforms. Market challenges become opportunities to demonstrate differentiation. Competitive pressure becomes the context for innovation. Leadership tests become platforms for modeling values. The very circumstances that intimidate others become your competitive advantage.

Emotional Regulation: The Secret Skill Under Pressure

Elite performers don't eliminate emotion. They regulate it. They understand that emotional intelligence isn't about suppressing feelings but managing them effectively. This capacity becomes particularly valuable during high-stakes business negotiations, leadership challenges, and market volatility.

They understand that pressure amplifies emotion, not logic. So they simplify their internal world. Breathing becomes intentional. Self-talk becomes short and grounded. Posture becomes strong. Attention narrows to what matters. These physiological and psychological practices create internal stability regardless of external circumstances.

Their internal checklist is simple:

What's my job?

What's in my control?

What does the aligned version of me do right now?

Pressure shrinks when clarity expands. The most effective response to increasing complexity is increasing simplicity. When markets become volatile, return to fundamentals. When competition intensifies, recommit to differentiation. When leadership challenges multiply, refocus on core values. Complexity in the environment demands simplicity in execution.

Pressure Is Not an Obstacle—It Is Preparation

Greatness is expensive. Pressure is the tuition. The development required for exceptional achievement doesn't happen in comfort—it emerges through challenge. This principle applies to individuals, teams, and organizations seeking meaningful impact.

You do not become unstoppable without learning to operate when stakes are high, fatigue is real, doubt is loud, risk is present, and consequences matter. Pressure is not trying to break you. Pressure is trying to build you. It strengthens decision-making capabilities, tests value systems, reveals character gaps, and develops resilience that becomes invaluable during future challenges.

Pressure is shaping the version of you that can handle the future you are asking for. If your destiny includes influence, leadership, or impact, pressure is not optional—it is training. The market challenges you face today are developing the capabilities you'll need tomorrow. The leadership tests you encounter are forming the character required for greater responsibility. The competitive pressure you experience is creating the differentiation necessary for sustainable advantage.

God never sends pressure to disqualify those He has called. He sends pressure to prepare them. The difficulties you encounter aren't evidence of abandonment but confirmation of assignment.

They're not punishment but preparation for the impact you're designed to create.

Why Pressure Is a Privilege

Pressure means you are trusted with responsibility. Pressure means the moment matters. Pressure means something significant is happening. People without purpose don't feel pressure—because nothing meaningful depends on them. The weight you feel is directly proportional to the impact you're positioned to create.

Pressure is a sign that growth is occurring. It indicates you're operating at the edge of your current capacity, where development happens. It confirms you're engaged in work that matters, decisions that have consequences, and leadership that affects others. The absence of pressure often signals the absence of meaningful contribution.

Avoiding pressure doesn't protect you. It postpones development. It delays the formation of capabilities essential for your next level of impact. It prevents the strengthening of decision-making processes required for greater responsibility. Organizations and individuals who systematically avoid pressure remain permanently underdeveloped, capable of handling only what's comfortable rather than what's consequential.

Training for Pressure Instead of Running from It

You don't rise to the occasion.

You fall to the level of your preparation.

That preparation is mental, emotional, and spiritual. It is built in private, during quiet reps, honest reflection, difficult conversations, disciplined habits, and identity work long before the moment arrives. It develops through intentional exposure to increasing levels of challenge, conscious evaluation of performance under pressure, and systematic improvement of response patterns.

Pressure doesn't reward luck.

Pressure rewards readiness. It favors those who have systematically prepared for its arrival through consistent development of capabilities, clarification of values, and strengthening of execution systems. The businesses that thrive during market disruption aren't lucky—they've built adaptable models, maintained financial discipline, and developed innovative cultures long before circumstances demanded them.

Reflection Questions

1. When was the last time pressure revealed something honest about you? What specific capabilities or limitations became visible during that high-stakes moment?

2. Do you collapse, survive, or attack under pressure—and why? What patterns have you noticed in your response to business challenges, leadership tests, or competitive pressure?

3. What belief about yourself needs to change so pressure activates rather than intimidates? How would this shift impact your leadership effectiveness and business performance?

4. What would shift if you interpreted pressure as confirmation instead of threat? How might this

reframing change your approach to market challenges and competitive intensity?

5. What habit, environment, or routine would strengthen your stability under pressure? What specific practice could you implement to improve your performance during high-stakes moments?

Closing Declaration

I no longer fear pressure.

I respect it.

Pressure does not threaten me—it reveals me.

I am not defined by the moment; the moment reveals who I've become.

I choose alignment over anxiety and identity over fear.

When the weight increases, my clarity increases.

Pressure is not punishment.

Pressure is preparation.

I am a Missionpreneur, and pressure is my privilege.

CHAPTER 10

FAITH AS THE OPERATING SYSTEM

Faith was never meant to be an accessory to leadership.

It was meant to govern it. The integration of faith into leadership creates a foundation that withstands market volatility, competitive pressures, and organizational challenges that inevitably arise in business.

Many leaders claim faith. Far fewer allow faith to decide. Faith that inspires but does not direct becomes sentiment rather than stewardship. Faith that comforts but does not confront becomes preference rather than obedience. This distinction separates leaders who merely survive from those who create lasting impact through principled decision-making.

For Missionpreneurs, faith is not merely what we believe.

Faith is how we operate. It represents the fundamental framework through which we filter opportunities, evaluate partnerships, and develop strategic initiatives that align with our core values and ultimate mission.

It informs how decisions are made, how pressure is handled, how people are treated, how money is stewarded, how opportunities are evaluated, and how legacy is protected. Faith, when properly ordered, is not emotional—it is operational. It becomes the invisible infrastructure supporting every visible action in our business and family leadership.

Why Faith So Often Fails at the Leadership Level

Most leaders do not reject faith. They compartmentalize it. This fragmentation creates inconsistency between stated values and operational decisions, undermining the very foundation of trust-based leadership.

Faith becomes personal rather than organizational. Private rather than procedural. Inspirational rather than instructional. Leaders pray for guidance, but default to instinct. They quote Scripture, but follow cultural trends. They ask God to bless decisions He was never invited to govern. This disconnect creates organizational confusion and erodes cultural clarity.

This separation feels harmless at first. But over time, it erodes clarity, authority, and longevity. Faith that does not guide decisions will never sustain legacy. It may decorate leadership, but it will not direct it. The consequences manifest in team disengagement, misaligned priorities, and diminished long-term impact.

Missionpreneurs understand this danger. They refuse to let faith remain symbolic. For them, faith becomes structural. We recognize that integrating faith throughout our decision-making processes creates consistency, builds trust, and establishes a foundation for multi-generational impact.

Faith as an Operating System, Not an Application

Think of faith the way you would think of technology. An application can be opened or closed. It is optional. An operating system, however, runs everything beneath the surface. It determines how inputs are processed and how outputs are produced. This distinction fundamentally changes how we approach business development and leadership.

When faith functions like an app, it is used selectively. It is overridden by urgency. It disappears under pressure. But when faith functions as the operating system, it informs every decision, shapes priorities, constrains behavior, and defines success. This systemic approach creates consistency that builds trust with stakeholders, team members, and family.

Missionpreneurs do not simply ask, Can we do this?

They ask, Should we do this before God? This higher standard of accountability transforms how we evaluate opportunities, structure partnerships, and develop strategic initiatives.

That question slows decisions—but it stabilizes legacy. The temporary cost in speed yields exponential returns in sustainability, integrity, and long-term impact that transcends quarterly performance metrics.

The Hidden Cost of Faithless Decisions

Every compromised legacy begins with a justification. Rarely is it dramatic. Often it sounds practical: cutting an ethical corner "just this once," avoiding a hard conversation to preserve peace, choosing speed over discernment, protecting reputation over righteousness. These seemingly minor compromises establish precedents that undermine organizational culture.

These moments rarely feel catastrophic in the moment. In fact, they often feel wise or efficient. But over time, they erode spiritual authority. You cannot build generational leadership on borrowed integrity. Each compromise weakens the foundation upon which sustainable success must be built.

Faithless decisions weaken the unseen foundation long before visible consequences appear. By the time performance metrics reflect the damage, cultural erosion has already occurred, requiring exponentially more resources to rebuild than would have been required to maintain integrity initially.

Biblical Leadership: Covenantal, Not Transactional

Modern leadership tends to be transactional. Decisions are evaluated through metrics of risk, return, exposure, and leverage. What's the upside? What's the downside? What's the ROI? While these questions have their place, they provide an incomplete framework for leadership that aims beyond quarterly results.

Biblical leadership, however, is covenantal. It asks deeper questions. Does this honor God? Does this align with calling? Does this protect those entrusted to us? These questions expand the decision-making framework beyond immediate outcomes to consider multi-generational impact, stakeholder well-being, and alignment with ultimate purpose.

Transactions build leverage. Covenants build trust. And trust is the currency of generational leadership. In a business environment increasingly focused on short-term metrics, covenant-based leadership creates distinctive competitive advantages through loyalty, commitment, and shared purpose.

Missionpreneurs choose covenant even when transactions appear more profitable, because covenant endures. We recognize that relationship-based leadership creates sustainable value that transcends market fluctuations and economic cycles.

When Faith Confronts Ambition

Ambition is not evil. Unsubmitted ambition is. The distinction lies in whether our aspirations serve our ego or our calling, whether they build personal kingdoms or contribute to eternal purposes.

When faith governs leadership, it will inevitably collide with ego-driven expansion, financial temptation, and opportunity without assignment. Just because something is good does not mean it is God. Just because something is available does not mean it is yours. This discernment protects us from pursuing opportunities that dilute our focus, compromise our values, or exceed our capacity.

Faith gives leaders permission to say no—even when yes would be easier, faster, or more profitable. That restraint is not weakness. It is wisdom. Strategic limitation often creates greater impact than unconstrained expansion, allowing us to excel in our specific assignment rather than diluting effectiveness across multiple ventures.

Biblical Example: Abraham and the Cost of Obedience

Abraham's leadership was not defined by speed or convenience. It was defined by obedience. He followed God into uncertainty, accepted delay without bitterness, and surrendered outcomes he deeply cared about. His leadership journey demonstrates that faith-based decisions often require patience, sacrifice, and trust in promises not yet fulfilled.

God trusted Abraham because Abraham trusted God enough to obey even when the future was unclear. That trust became the foundation for generational blessing. Abraham's willingness to prioritize obedience over immediate gratification established a legacy that continues thousands of years later—a powerful model for Missionpreneurs seeking multi-generational impact.

Faith does not guarantee clarity before action.

Faith produces clarity through obedience. This principle transforms how we approach strategic planning, risk management, and organizational development—recognizing that some clarity only comes through faithful execution, not exhaustive analysis.

The Faith Decision Filter

Missionpreneurs evaluate major decisions through a consistent filter. This systematic approach ensures alignment between our values and our actions, creating coherence that builds trust with stakeholders, team members, and family.

They begin with obedience—does this align with biblical truth? They consider assignment—is this ours to carry or simply available? They evaluate impact—how will this affect those under our care? They examine integrity—would we still choose this if no one saw it? And they ask about generational effect—what precedent does this set? This comprehensive framework transforms how opportunities are evaluated and resources are allocated.

Any decision that fails this filter may still succeed temporarily—but it will not sustain legacy. Short-term gains achieved through compromised decision-making inevitably create long-term liabilities that undermine sustainable success and generational impact.

Faith Establishes Authority

Spiritual authority is not positional; it is relational. Leaders lose authority when private life contradicts public voice, convictions fluctuate under pressure, or obedience becomes selective. Authority flows from alignment, not assertion—from consistent character rather than positional power.

Faith-first leaders operate from alignment rather than appearance. That alignment produces quiet authority—authority that does not need validation or enforcement. This authentic leadership creates influence that extends beyond organizational boundaries and positional limitations.

People trust leaders whose faith governs decisions, not just speeches. This trust-based influence creates organizational cultures characterized by commitment rather than compliance, innovation rather than fear, and purpose rather than mere productivity.

Prayer as Strategy, Not Escape

Prayer is often misunderstood. Some leaders use prayer to delay decisions, avoid confrontation, or mask fear. Missionpreneurs treat prayer differently. Prayer becomes strategic alignment. It serves as the critical connection point between our limited perspective and God's unlimited wisdom.

Prayer clarifies timing. Prayer exposes motive. Prayer anchors conviction. Prayer is not retreat; it is reconnaissance. It prepares leaders to act with clarity rather than react with emotion. This strategic approach to prayer transforms it from a religious ritual into a leadership discipline that enhances decision-making.

When faith governs prayer, prayer strengthens leadership rather than replacing it. It becomes the foundation for courageous action rather than an excuse for passivity, informing strategic planning, team development, and resource allocation with wisdom beyond human capability.

Faith in the Family System

Faith that does not govern the family will not govern the enterprise. Children do not inherit beliefs; they inherit patterns. When faith is inconsistent, performative, or optional at home, the next generation learns to compartmentalize as well. This disconnection undermines the intergenerational transfer of both values and vision.

Legacy faith is caught before it is taught. What you practice privately will always outweigh what you preach publicly. The alignment between family culture and organizational culture creates consistency that builds trust, reinforces values, and establishes patterns that can be sustainably transferred to the next generation.

The Cost of Obedience

Operating by faith is expensive. It costs comfort, approval, and control. But disobedience costs far more—credibility, authority, and longevity. This recognition transforms how we evaluate decisions, understanding that immediate comfort often comes at the expense of lasting impact.

Missionpreneurs choose obedience not because it is easy, but because it is durable. Obedience builds foundations that pressure cannot shake. While market conditions fluctuate and business models evolve, principled leadership creates sustainable competitive advantages through trust, consistency, and purpose-driven decision-making.

Faith Builds Endurance

Faith accomplishes what talent alone cannot. It sustains leaders through adversity, anchors organizations during transition, and provides clarity when outcomes are uncertain. This resilience creates stability through market volatility, competitive disruption, and organizational challenges.

Talent builds momentum.

Faith sustains mission. This distinction explains why many talented leaders create impressive short-term results but struggle to build lasting legacy. Sustainable impact requires both capability and conviction—skill and steadfastness working in tandem.

When seasons grow long and pressure intensifies, faith remains when excitement disappears. This endurance enables Missionpreneurs to maintain focus during difficult seasons, persist through obstacles, and create multi-generational impact that transcends immediate circumstances.

Reflection Questions

1. Where in my leadership has faith inspired but not governed? What specific decisions have been made without applying faith-based discernment?
2. What decisions have I made from urgency rather than obedience? How have those decisions affected organizational culture and team trust?
3. Where might ambition be outrunning discernment? What opportunities should be reconsidered through the lens of assignment rather than availability?
4. How does my private life reinforce—or undermine—my public leadership? Where are the gaps between what I profess and what I practice?
5. What would change if faith truly operated as my leadership foundation? How would decision-making processes, resource allocation, and strategic planning be transformed?

Closing Declaration

Faith is not what I declare when life is calm.

It is what governs when pressure rises. It becomes the stabilizing force when market conditions fluctuate, competition intensifies, or organizational challenges emerge.

I refuse compartmentalized belief and selective obedience.

Faith directs my decisions, shapes my leadership, and anchors my legacy.

I will build on obedience, not urgency.

I choose covenant over convenience. This commitment transforms how I evaluate opportunities, develop partnerships, and allocate resources.

Faith is not the accessory of my leadership.

Faith is the operating system. It forms the foundational framework through which every decision is filtered, every relationship is managed, and every strategy is developed.

I am a Missionpreneur, and I lead from obedience.

CHAPTER 11

DISCIPLINE: THE REAL FLEX

Mastering Consistency Without Burnout

Everybody loves motivation.

Everybody loves excitement.

Everybody loves momentum.

But motivation doesn't build champions—discipline does. This fundamental truth separates those who achieve lasting success from those who merely experience temporary wins. The path to extraordinary achievement isn't paved with fleeting enthusiasm but with reliable, consistent action.

Motivation screams at the beginning. Discipline whispers every day. Motivation feels good. Discipline feels necessary. Motivation is emotional. Discipline is foundational. While motivation provides the initial spark, discipline supplies the sustainable fuel that powers long-term achievement and meaningful progress.

It's easy to chase your goals when you're excited. The real question is this: Who are you when you're not excited? This question reveals the true character of a Missionpreneur who understands that results don't materialize from occasional bursts of inspiration but from steady, reliable execution regardless of circumstances.

Greatness does not belong to the most hyped. It belongs to the most consistent. In a world obsessed with overnight success stories, the reality remains that sustainable achievement follows a much quieter, more deliberate path marked by daily commitment rather than dramatic moments.

People get praised for talent, celebrated for wins, and applauded for outcomes. But the truth nobody likes to say out loud is this: the most successful people in the world do not have the most talent—they have the most discipline. Behind every "overnight success" stands years of invisible work, countless hours of practice, and unwavering commitment to excellence when nobody was watching.

Discipline is the invisible advantage. It is quiet, unglamorous, and relentless. And over time, it outperforms everything else. While others chase recognition and validation, the disciplined Missionpreneur focuses on building systems and habits that deliver consistent results regardless of external circumstances or emotional fluctuations.

Why Discipline Matters More Than Hype

A person who trains only when they feel like it will always lose to the person who trains even when they don't. A person who performs only when the energy is high will always lose to the person who can execute on demand. A person who acts based on mood will always lose to the person who acts based on mission. The marketplace rewards reliability over sporadic brilliance.

Discipline is the difference between I hope I succeed and I refuse not to. This mindset distinction transforms wishful thinking into strategic certainty, replacing the passive stance of hope with the active position of determination. The disciplined Missionpreneur doesn't leave achievement to chance but creates systems that make success inevitable.

When the world loses motivation, disciplined people keep moving. That gap—between who quits and who continues—is where destiny is built. This persistence through difficulty becomes a competitive advantage that compounds over time, creating distance between those who maintain momentum and those who surrender to resistance.

Hype creates crowds. Discipline creates leaders. While attention often flows to those who make the most noise, sustainable influence belongs to those who deliver consistent value. The disciplined Missionpreneur understands that leadership isn't conferred by position but earned through reliable execution and consistent character.

Biblical Example: Daniel — Discipline That Creates Influence

Daniel did not rise because of luck or timing. He rose because of discipline. His story demonstrates how consistent excellence positions a person for extraordinary influence regardless of external circumstances. Daniel's life reveals the power of unwavering commitment to principles and practices aligned with divine purpose.

He prayed consistently. He studied consistently. He honored God consistently. He lived with integrity consistently—regardless of whether it was popular, convenient, or safe. Even when threatened with death, Daniel did not abandon discipline. This level of commitment transcends mere habit and reveals the power of discipline anchored in unshakable conviction.

That was not reckless faith. That was alignment. Daniel understood that true discipline flows from identity and purpose rather than mere willpower or external pressure. His actions weren't separated from his beliefs but were the natural expression of who he was at his core.

Daniel's discipline positioned him for influence across multiple administrations, cultures, and crises. His consistency outlasted political shifts, pressure, and persecution. While others compromised to accommodate changing circumstances, Daniel's steadfast adherence to his principles made him indispensable even to those who didn't share his beliefs.

Purpose without discipline produces frustration.

Discipline without purpose produces burnout.

Purpose with discipline produces influence.

Why Most People Struggle With Discipline

Most people think they have a discipline problem. In reality, they have an identity problem. This misdiagnosis leads to focusing on behavioral tactics rather than addressing the fundamental beliefs that drive consistent action. True transformation begins with reimagining who you are, not just what you do.

When someone believes, I'm inconsistent, I always fall off, I can't stick with anything, their brain will subconsciously protect that identity by sabotaging discipline. The failure is not moral—it's neurological and psychological. Our nervous system works tirelessly to maintain congruence between our actions and our self-concept, even when that self-concept limits our potential.

Discipline fails when it contradicts identity. Attempting to force behaviors that conflict with how we see ourselves creates internal resistance that eventually undermines even the most determined efforts. Sustainable discipline requires aligning actions with a clear, compelling self-image.

But when a person believes, I'm a finisher, I show up on bad days, I do what needs to be done, I'm reliable to my calling, discipline stops feeling forced. It becomes natural. The same actions that once required tremendous willpower now flow from an internal sense of congruence and self-expression.

Discipline isn't about pain tolerance.

Discipline is about identity tolerance.

Your nervous system will always default to who you believe you are. This neurological reality means that sustainable discipline requires not just behavioral change but identity transformation. The Missionpreneur who masters this principle builds consistency from the inside out rather than relying solely on external systems and accountability.

Discipline Without Burnout: The Misunderstood Secret

Average people believe discipline means doing more. Elite performers understand discipline means doing what matters longer. This distinction separates those who exhaust themselves with busyness from those who create lasting impact through focused, strategic persistence. Effective discipline isn't about quantity but quality and longevity.

Burnout does not come from hard work. Burnout comes from misaligned work. You get exhausted when you are chasing the wrong reward, operating from the wrong identity, performing for approval, or trying to live someone else's calling. The disciplined Missionpreneur recognizes that sustainability requires alignment between actions and authentic purpose.

When you are aligned with mission, discipline gives energy instead of draining it. It builds confidence instead of resentment. It creates momentum instead of depletion. This counterintuitive reality explains why some people find renewed vitality through consistent effort while others collapse under the same demands.

The right work does not exhaust you—it strengthens you. When discipline flows from genuine calling rather than external pressure, it becomes regenerative rather than depleting. The key to sustainable discipline isn't reducing commitment but ensuring that commitment serves your authentic purpose and leverages your unique design.

Discipline Is a Skill, Not a Personality Trait

People love to excuse inconsistency by labeling themselves. I'm just not disciplined. That's not my personality. I don't have that mindset. These self-limiting beliefs create artificial barriers to growth and provide convenient explanations for patterns that could be changed through deliberate practice.

Those statements feel honest, but they are inaccurate. They confuse current capacity with permanent limitation and mistake temporary struggles for fixed character traits. The disciplined Missionpreneur recognizes that consistency is developed rather than discovered.

Discipline is not genetic. It is trained. Like any skill, it responds to deliberate practice, strategic reinforcement, and progressive challenge. Understanding discipline as a trainable capacity rather than an innate trait opens the door to growth regardless of natural inclination or past performance.

It grows through small daily repetitions, honoring commitments to yourself, and doing what you said you would do long after emotion fades. This incremental approach makes discipline accessible to anyone willing to start where they are and build capacity through consistent practice rather than heroic effort.

Discipline is not about never missing a day. Discipline is about never quitting. This distinction liberates us from perfectionism while maintaining the commitment to progress. True discipline isn't measured by flawless execution but by the capacity to recover from disruption and maintain direction despite inevitable setbacks.

The Three Levels of Discipline

At the beginner level, discipline depends on motivation. Action happens only when energy is high. Consistency is accidental. At this stage, performance fluctuates dramatically based on external circumstances and internal feelings. The beginner requires optimal conditions to maintain momentum.

At the intermediate level, discipline becomes a choice. Action happens whether emotion cooperates or not. Consistency becomes possible. This stage represents significant progress as the individual develops the capacity to override temporary resistance and maintain direction despite fluctuating motivation.

At the elite level, discipline becomes identity. Action happens because it reflects who the person is. Consistency becomes inevitable. At this advanced stage, disciplined behavior flows naturally from a transformed self-concept rather than requiring conscious decision or emotional management.

Beginners chase feelings.

Intermediate performers chase standards.

Elite performers embody identity.

The shift from I have to → I choose to → this is who I am is the foundation of greatness. This progression represents the evolution from external compliance to internal commitment to complete integration. The disciplined Missionpreneur intentionally cultivates this development rather than remaining at the initial stages of motivation-dependent action.

The Small-Action Multiplier

The world idolizes dramatic transformation, but real growth is built through boring consistency. One hour every day beats four hours once a week. Learning every month forever beats ten books in one burst. Small habits compound into unstoppable momentum. This principle of incremental accumulation creates results that appear extraordinary but are actually the product of ordinary actions performed with unusual consistency.

Big discipline is not built in big moments.

Big discipline is built in small actions done without negotiation.

Consistency is a multiplier. It turns ordinary effort into extraordinary outcomes. The disciplined Missionpreneur understands that remarkable achievement doesn't require remarkable talent but rather remarkable persistence applied to fundamental practices. This approach makes excellence accessible through commitment rather than genius.

How Discipline Builds Confidence and Self-Respect

There is a reason undisciplined people struggle with confidence. Every broken promise to yourself weakens self-trust. And there is a reason disciplined people walk with quiet confidence. Every kept promise strengthens identity. This reciprocal relationship between action and self-perception creates either an upward spiral of increasing capability or a downward spiral of diminishing belief.

Self-belief is not built through hype or affirmation. It is built through integrity with yourself. While positive thinking has value, genuine confidence emerges from a proven track record of following through on commitments, especially when those commitments were challenging. The disciplined Missionpreneur builds confidence through consistent action rather than mental manipulation.

If you want to believe in yourself again, don't start with motivation. Start with commitments. Start with repetition. Start with small wins. This practical approach rebuilds self-trust through tangible evidence rather than aspirational thinking. Each completed commitment, no matter how small, creates momentum toward renewed confidence.

Discipline restores dignity. Beyond practical outcomes, consistent discipline reconnects us with our inherent capacity for growth and achievement. It replaces shame and self-doubt with the quiet assurance that comes from knowing you can depend on yourself to follow through despite obstacles.

Structuring Discipline for Sustainability

You do not need more motivation. You need more structure. This insight shifts focus from emotional management to environmental design. The disciplined Missionpreneur creates systems that make consistency possible rather than relying on fluctuating inspiration to drive action.

Discipline thrives when it is scheduled, small enough to sustain, tracked for evidence, protected from negotiation, and attached to purpose. If discipline is optional, it will always lose to emotion. If discipline is aligned with calling, it will endure. These practical elements transform abstract commitment into concrete action that can withstand the inevitable challenges of implementation.

Structure removes the daily decision. Once the decision is made, execution becomes automatic. This principle of decision minimization conserves willpower and reduces the cognitive load associated with consistent action. By establishing clear systems and protocols, the disciplined Missionpreneur eliminates the friction that often derails good intentions.

Discipline Is How You Prepare for Pressure

Pressure exposes habits. When stress increases, people do not rise to the occasion—they fall to the level of their discipline. Discipline is what allows people to execute when motivation disappears, when confidence wavers, and when outcomes matter. This reality explains why some individuals maintain performance under pressure while others collapse despite similar capability.

You don't build discipline for pressure.

You build discipline because of pressure.

Discipline trains obedience to purpose when emotion is uncooperative. This capacity to maintain direction despite internal resistance becomes invaluable during challenging circumstances when feelings naturally push toward comfort rather than commitment. The disciplined Missionpreneur develops this skill deliberately rather than hoping it will materialize when needed.

Discipline as a Legacy Trait

Discipline is one of the most transferable leadership traits. Children, teams, and organizations do not inherit motivation— they inherit patterns. What you do consistently teaches others what matters. This principle of behavioral transmission means that the disciplined Missionpreneur influences others not primarily through instruction but through demonstration.

Discipline creates cultures that last beyond leadership transitions. Motivation builds moments. Discipline builds institutions. While charismatic leadership can create temporary enthusiasm, only embedded discipline can sustain excellence across generations and through changing circumstances. This distinction explains why some organizations thrive long-term while others collapse after initial success.

Legacy is sustained consistency over time. The disciplined Missionpreneur recognizes that lasting impact doesn't come from occasional brilliance but from reliable excellence maintained across seasons and circumstances. This perspective transforms daily discipline from mundane routine into meaningful contribution to a larger story.

Reflection Questions

1. Where in my life am I motivated but not disciplined? What specific areas show enthusiasm without consistent follow-through?
2. How would my results change if discipline became part of my identity rather than effort? What would be different in my business, relationships, and personal development?
3. What small daily commitment would rebuild my self-trust fastest? Which consistent action would create the most significant momentum toward renewed confidence?

4. Where have I been operating from hype instead of purpose? In what areas have I substituted excitement for alignment?

5. What habit would change everything if I refused to negotiate with it? Which consistent practice would create the most substantial competitive advantage for my mission?

Closing Declaration

I refuse to build my life on motivation alone.

I choose discipline.

I show up when I feel like it—and when I don't.

I honor commitments because they shape my identity.

Consistency is my advantage.

Purpose fuels my discipline.

Discipline protects my destiny.

I am not ruled by emotion.

I am anchored by assignment.

I am a Missionpreneur, and discipline is my real flex.

CHAPTER 12

FAMILY IS YOUR FIRST ORGANIZATION

Why Private Stewardship Determines Public Legacy

Before you ever led a team,

before you built a business,

before you carried influence,

you were entrusted with a family.

Not as a reward.

As a responsibility.

Family is not the backdrop of leadership. It is the proving ground. No legacy survives when the first organization is neglected, unmanaged, or assumed. What is tolerated at home will eventually surface in public leadership. Private disorder always produces public instability—just later, and at a higher cost. The patterns established in family relationships inevitably transfer to business relationships, whether intentionally or unconsciously.

The Most Ignored Leadership System

Many leaders obsess over organizational charts, bylaws, boards, performance metrics, and succession plans. They invest enormous energy into governing institutions while leaving their most influential system undefined. They meticulously document corporate policies yet operate their households on unspoken assumptions and emotional reactions.

Family becomes assumed instead of structured. Emotional instead of intentional. Reactive instead of governed. The very system that shapes a leader's foundational habits, values, and relational patterns remains the least deliberately designed.

Leadership principles are applied everywhere—except where they matter most. This disconnect creates a fundamental integrity gap that undermines sustainable legacy building at its core.

What you permit in your family will eventually undermine what you lead publicly. You cannot compartmentalize leadership. Integrity leaks. The private compromises you rationalize will inevitably manifest in your public decisions, often at the most critical moments of leadership testing.

Why Family Breakdown Destroys Legacy

Legacy rarely collapses in boardrooms.

It collapses in living rooms.

When family leadership is neglected, resentment replaces respect. Silence replaces clarity. Entitlement replaces responsibility. Public success may temporarily mask private fractures, but it never heals them. The organizational structure you build cannot withstand the foundational cracks forming beneath it.

Unresolved family tension eventually surfaces as power struggles, financial conflict, moral compromise, and generational division. You cannot hand off leadership where trust has eroded. You cannot build institutions strong enough to survive what the family refuses to confront. The mission-driven enterprise you've created will inevitably reflect the health—or dysfunction—of your primary organizational system.

Private avoidance always becomes public failure. The conversations postponed, the boundaries unenforced, the expectations uncommunicated—these seemingly small family governance gaps eventually undermine even the most carefully constructed business legacy.

Family Is Not a Safe Space—It Is a Formation Space

Modern culture treats family primarily as a place of comfort. Scripture treats family as a place of formation. Comfort avoids conflict. Formation requires it. This fundamental misalignment creates leaders who expect their families to serve as emotional refuges rather than character forges.

Missionpreneurs understand this distinction. Love without accountability breeds chaos. Authority without clarity breeds resentment. Provision without responsibility breeds entitlement.

Each of these imbalances creates organizational dysfunction that inevitably transfers from family systems to business systems.

Biblical family leadership is neither harsh nor passive. It is ordered. Order does not eliminate love—it protects it. Structure doesn't diminish relationship—it creates the secure framework within which authentic relationships can flourish. The most loving family leaders establish clear expectations precisely because they value family relationships too highly to leave them vulnerable to the chaos of assumption.

The Leader's First Governance Assignment

If you can lead strangers but not your household, something is misaligned. The issue is not capacity. It is priority. Many leaders invest their best strategic thinking, clearest communication, and most disciplined execution in their businesses while giving their families emotional leftovers and reactive management.

Family leadership requires the same fundamentals as any healthy organization: clear expectations, defined roles, consistent standards, and loving accountability. None of these diminish relationship. They stabilize it. The governance principles that build sustainable businesses also build sustainable families—applied with appropriate contextual wisdom.

Leaders who avoid structure at home often justify it with emotion. In reality, they fear discomfort. But discomfort avoided today becomes dysfunction tomorrow. The temporary peace purchased through avoidance always costs more than the temporary tension created through clarity. Missionpreneurs recognize that family governance is not optional—it is foundational.

Biblical Example: Eli — Influence Without Governance

Scripture gives a sobering warning through the life of Eli. Eli was a priest—spiritually influential and publicly respected. But he failed to govern his household. His sons abused authority, violated trust, and corrupted the priesthood. They transformed their father's spiritual legacy into an opportunity for exploitation.

Eli confronted them verbally, but never enforced consequences. His leadership stopped at correction and never reached governance. His words communicated standards, but his actions communicated tolerance. The gap between what he professed and what he permitted undermined his entire legacy.

God judged Eli not for ignorance, but for tolerance. The divine assessment was not that Eli failed to know better, but that he failed to act on what he knew. His public position could not compensate for his private negligence.

Eli's story reveals a painful truth: spiritual influence cannot compensate for domestic negligence. Leadership failure at home eventually disqualifies leadership everywhere else. Modern missionpreneurs face the same fundamental challenge—building governance systems that align private stewardship with public mission.

The Myth of "They'll Figure It Out"

Many leaders assume family members will naturally understand values, expectations, roles, and boundaries. They won't. What seems obvious to the founder remains opaque to those who didn't build the system. The unspoken rules that govern your decision-making are invisible to others until articulated.

Assumption breeds confusion. Confusion breeds conflict. Anything important enough to pass on is important enough to explain clearly. The mission, values, and operational principles that guide your leadership decisions must be explicitly taught, not implicitly absorbed.

Silence does not preserve peace. It postpones conflict. The conversations avoided today create the crises managed tomorrow. Missionpreneurs recognize that clarity is kindness—the most loving gift they can offer their families is transparent expectations aligned with consistent action.

Family Governance Is Not Control

Governance is not micromanagement. Governance is clarity. It creates the framework within which freedom can flourish safely. Just as business governance establishes parameters that enable innovation rather than restricting it, family governance creates boundaries that enable relationship rather than controlling it.

Healthy governance answers questions before emotion takes over: who decides what, who is accountable to whom, how conflict is resolved, and what happens when standards are violated. Without governance, emotion becomes the CEO. Decision-making becomes reactive rather than principled, inconsistent rather than reliable.

Emotion is a terrible leader. It is reactive, inconsistent, and biased. Governance protects relationships by removing guesswork. It transforms subjective feelings into objective standards, replacing

"I feel" with "we agreed." This shift from emotional reaction to principled response creates the stability essential for both family harmony and business continuity.

The Missionpreneur Family Model

Missionpreneur families are built with intentional order, dignity, and purpose. They are neither authoritarian nor permissive. They are structured with care. The governance model balances clear authority with genuine respect, establishing parameters that protect relationships while promoting growth.

Faith leads by example, not enforcement. Values are spoken, written, and reinforced. Responsibility precedes privilege. Accountability is consistent and fair. Honor flows both directions. These principles create a family culture that naturally aligns with the organizational culture missionpreneurs seek to establish in their enterprises.

Authority without love hardens hearts. Love without authority weakens legacy. Missionpreneurs balance both. They recognize that leadership requires both strength and tenderness—the courage to establish standards and the compassion to restore those who fail. This balanced approach creates resilient family systems capable of sustaining multi-generational impact.

When Family and Enterprise Collide

One of the most destructive legacy mistakes is mixing family access, business authority, and financial benefit without boundaries. When family roles automatically confer business positions, both systems become compromised. Relationship expectations conflict with performance requirements, creating impossible tensions.

Love does not replace qualification. Relationship does not replace responsibility. Affection does not equal readiness. When these distinctions blur, both family harmony and business effectiveness suffer. The missionpreneur must establish clear separation between family membership and organizational leadership.

Missionpreneurs refuse to confuse bloodline with leadership. They protect both family and mission by defining boundaries early. Clear separation prevents resentment later. Family members understand that business roles must be earned through competence, not inherited through connection. This clarity preserves both the integrity of the enterprise and the authenticity of family relationships.

Children as Apprentices, Not Heirs

Inheritance without preparation is sabotage disguised as blessing. When the next generation receives authority, resources, or responsibility without corresponding character development, failure becomes inevitable. The very assets intended to empower them instead expose their unreadiness.

Children are not entitled to leadership; they are invited into training. Missionpreneur families emphasize work ethic before wealth, character before control, and competence before authority. They create developmental pathways that test and strengthen the next generation before entrusting them with significant responsibility.

Leadership is earned through stewardship, not assumed by birthright. This principle protects both the enterprise from unprepared leadership and the next generation from premature responsibility. True legacy building requires the discipline to develop leaders, not merely designate them. Missionpreneurs invest in formation before transition.

The Silent Legacy Killer

The greatest threat to legacy is not rebellion.

It is silence.

Silence about expectations. Silence about money. Silence about roles. Silence about succession. Silence about standards. These communication gaps create assumption chasms that eventually swallow even the most promising legacies. The conversations avoided become the conflicts inherited.

Unspoken expectations become unmet expectations. Unmet expectations produce bitterness. Clarity prevents conflict before it forms. The missionpreneur's responsibility includes creating communication systems that transform implicit assumptions into explicit agreements, replacing dangerous silence with productive dialogue.

Family Governance Audit

Every Missionpreneur must eventually face hard questions. Are family values written or assumed? Are roles defined or fluid? Is accountability consistent or emotional? Are financial expectations transparent? Is succession discussed openly? These governance fundamentals determine whether your legacy will transfer intact or fragment under pressure.

Any unclear answer represents generational risk. The governance gaps you tolerate today become the legacy fractures your successors manage tomorrow. Conducting regular family governance audits allows you to address structural weaknesses before they create systemic failures.

Leading With Strength and Tenderness

Family leadership requires courage to confront, wisdom to listen, humility to repent, and discipline to stay consistent. Authority must be strong enough to lead and tender enough to restore. This balanced leadership approach creates secure attachment rather than anxious compliance or rebellious detachment.

This balance does not happen by accident. It is practiced. The missionpreneur must intentionally develop both strength and tenderness, cultivating the discernment to know which response each situation requires. This leadership maturity creates family systems resilient enough to weather both success and failure without losing core identity.

Why Heaven Evaluates Private Leadership First

The world applauds what you build publicly. Heaven evaluates what you steward privately. This eternal perspective realigns priorities, revealing that your most significant leadership impact may occur within your home rather than your organization. The disciples you develop most profoundly may be those who share your name.

Family is not a side responsibility. It is the first leadership assignment. If the family fractures, the legacy fractures. Public success never redeems private failure. The organizational monuments you build cannot compensate for the relational wreckage you create. True legacy integrates both.

Missionpreneurs understand this ordering. They do not sacrifice family on the altar of influence. They build influence on the foundation of family stewardship. They recognize that their most enduring impact flows through the leaders they develop at home before extending to those they develop elsewhere. Private faithfulness precedes public fruitfulness.

Reflection Questions

1. Where have I applied leadership principles publicly but avoided them privately? What specific governance practices would strengthen my family system?
2. What assumptions exist in my family that should be clarified? Which unspoken expectations create the greatest risk of future conflict?
3. Where is silence creating risk in our family culture? What conversation am I avoiding that, if addressed now, would prevent significant problems later?
4. How am I preparing the next generation rather than protecting comfort? What developmental experiences am I creating that build leadership capacity in my children?

5. What boundary or conversation is overdue? What specific step will I take this week to address it?

Closing Declaration

I refuse to build a public legacy on private neglect.

Family is my first organization and my first assignment.

I will lead with clarity, love, and courage.

I will confront early, communicate clearly, and steward faithfully.

What I model privately will sustain what I build publicly.

The world may applaud my influence.

But I will answer for my stewardship.

I am a Missionpreneur, and my legacy begins at home.

CHAPTER 13

FOCUS UNDER FIRE

Thinking Clearly and Performing Under Chaos

Anyone can focus when life is calm.

Anyone can execute when everything is going right.

Anyone can dominate when nothing is going wrong.

The real test of a high performer is not how they behave when they are comfortable—it is how they behave when they are surrounded by chaos. True excellence reveals itself not during periods of stability, but in moments of intense pressure when everything seems to be falling apart. This distinction separates ordinary performers from extraordinary achievers in every field of human endeavor.

When momentum shifts.

When expectations rise.

When the crowd gets loud.

When mistakes happen.

When pressure attacks the mind.

When the situation feels out of control.

That is the moment where identity reveals itself. These crucible moments strip away pretense and expose our fundamental character. They reveal not just what we do, but who we truly are at our core. For the Missionpreneur, these moments of truth define our legacy.

Chaos does not change people.

Chaos exposes them.

Distractions do not destroy focus.

They reveal the strength—or weakness—of the focus that was built beforehand.

Anyone can concentrate when nothing is demanding attention.

Champions concentrate when everything is demanding attention.

Chaos Is Not the Enemy—Confusion Is

Most people misidentify the enemy in high-pressure moments. They think chaos is the problem. It isn't. Confusion is. This critical distinction transforms how we approach challenging situations. Chaos is simply an environmental condition—confusion is a mental state that surrenders our power.

Pressure is not the enemy. Panic is.

Obstacles are not the enemy. Overreaction is.

Chaos only becomes dangerous when it overwhelms the mind to the point where thinking collapses. When clarity disappears, confidence disappears. When confidence disappears, execution breaks down. This cascading failure pattern explains why talented individuals and organizations crumble under pressure despite having all the necessary capabilities.

The solution is not eliminating chaos.

The solution is developing clarity that cannot be shaken by chaos.

When the outside world gets loud, the inner world must become quiet. That is the dividing line between people who survive moments and people who seize them. This inner quietude becomes a competitive advantage in business, leadership, and life—allowing decisive action while others remain paralyzed by uncertainty.

The world gets loud.

The warrior gets calm.

Biblical Example: Jesus Sleeping in the Storm

One of the most revealing leadership moments in Scripture happens on a boat during a violent storm. The disciples panic. They scramble. They assume destruction is imminent. Their reaction demonstrates the natural human response to overwhelming circumstances—fear, anxiety, and catastrophic thinking.

Jesus sleeps.

The storm itself was not the lesson. The response to the storm was. This profound contrast illustrates the power of internal peace amidst external chaos. As Missionpreneurs, we are called to embody this same unshakable presence in our business and leadership roles.

Everyone experienced the same chaos. Only one person maintained focus. Nothing outside the boat was calm. Everything inside Jesus was calm. His response wasn't based on different circumstances but on a different internal reality—one anchored in complete confidence and clarity of purpose.

This is elite performance psychology in spiritual form.

You do not need calm conditions to remain calm.

You need a calm identity to dominate any condition.

That identity is not developed in the storm. It is revealed by it. The preparation happens in the quiet moments of intentional identity formation, spiritual discipline, and mental training long before the crisis arrives.

What Chaos Does to the Brain

When the brain senses danger—real or imagined—it activates the fight, flight, or freeze response. This is biological survival wiring. Under pressure, symptoms appear rapidly: overthinking, tunnel vision, emotional flooding, muscle tension, irrational decision-making, and panic. These neurological responses helped our ancestors survive physical threats but can sabotage modern performance in business, leadership, and critical decision-making.

Performance collapses not because ability vanished, but because perception changed. The skills remain intact, but the brain's interpretation of the situation transforms dramatically, blocking access to those capabilities when they're needed most.

High performers train their nervous system to interpret pressure as challenge, not threat. This single shift changes everything. Threat triggers panic. Challenge triggers confidence. Elite performers in business, sports, military operations, and crisis management all demonstrate this same fundamental mental reframing.

The situation does not change.

The meaning of the situation does.

And meaning determines performance. This principle applies equally to navigating market volatility, managing team crises, making high-stakes decisions, or executing in moments of opportunity. The meaning we assign creates either limitation or possibility.

Why People Choke Under Pressure

People do not choke because they forget how to perform. They choke because their focus moves from execution to outcome. This subtle shift in attention creates a cascade of performance-destroying mental processes that can derail even the most prepared individuals and teams.

Outcome-based thoughts activate anxiety. What if I fail? What if I miss? What will people think? What if this ruins everything? These forward-projecting concerns trigger stress hormones, muscle tension, and cognitive interference that directly impair performance capabilities.

Those thoughts pull the brain into the future, where fear lives. The future is inherently uncertain, making it fertile ground for anxiety, doubt, and catastrophic thinking. This future-focus removes us from our power zone—the present moment.

Execution-based thoughts anchor the brain in the present. What's my job? Where's my target? What does the best version of me do right now? These process-focused questions activate competence, confidence, and clarity by directing attention to actionable elements within our control.

The moment focus shifts from fear of consequences to responsibility of action, performance stabilizes. This mental pivot transforms anxiety into purposeful energy and converts pressure into productive focus—a critical skill for Missionpreneurs facing high-stakes decisions and opportunities.

You do not rise under pressure by thinking harder.

You rise by thinking simpler.

The Three Focus Zones

The mind can only live in three places. Understanding these time dimensions is crucial for maintaining peak performance under pressure and making optimal decisions in complex situations.

Some people stay trapped in the past, replaying mistakes and regrets. That creates hesitation. Others drift into the future, imagining outcomes and expectations. That creates anxiety. Both mental time travels remove us from the only place where we have genuine power and agency.

Elite performers live in the present. They develop sophisticated mental disciplines to continually return their focus to the immediate moment, regardless of distractions, pressures, or stakes.

This present-moment mastery becomes their competitive advantage.

The present is the only place where action exists. The present is where identity expresses itself. The present is where control lives. Every decision, every action, every moment of impact happens exclusively in the present—making it the only zone where true performance excellence can emerge.

Champions do not replay errors.

They do not predict disaster.

They do not argue with outcomes.

They lock into one moment, one task, one identity—right now. This singular focus creates extraordinary clarity and unleashes their full capabilities without the interference of past regrets or future anxieties.

The Discipline of Present-Moment Dominance

Present-moment focus is not accidental. It is trained. High performers do not wait for focus to appear. They force it through discipline. This intentional approach to mental performance distinguishes elite achievers across every domain of human excellence, from business leadership to athletic achievement to crisis management.

They understand that clarity is not emotional—it is mechanical. Focus is not a feeling. It is a process. This perspective transforms focus from a mysterious state that comes and goes unpredictably into a reliable capability that can be systematically developed and deployed.

That process must be practiced before pressure arrives. Just as physical skills deteriorate without consistent training, mental focus requires deliberate practice in progressively challenging environments. For the Missionpreneur, this means intentionally developing focus disciplines during normal operations that will sustain performance during inevitable crises.

Four Tools Elite Performers Use Under Fire

When chaos shows up, elite performers default to trained responses. These tactical focus tools have been tested in the most demanding environments, from special operations to championship athletics to high-stakes business negotiations. They work because they directly address the neurological and psychological mechanisms that govern human performance.

First, they regulate breath. Breathing patterns signal safety or threat to the brain. Slow, controlled breath calms the nervous system and restores rational thought. A simple pattern—in four seconds, hold two, out six—can reset clarity almost instantly. This physiological intervention interrupts the stress cascade and reestablishes cognitive control.

Second, they fixate visually. The brain cannot obsess about chaos when it is anchored to a single visual target. A mark, a line, a cue—anything that pulls attention into the present moment. This visual anchoring technique prevents attention fragmentation and maintains processing capacity for the task at hand.

Third, they issue an identity command. This is a short phrase that triggers confidence and alignment. I'm built for this. This is mine. I do this. These identity statements activate deep neural pathways associated with capability, confidence, and purpose—

instantly reconnecting performers with their strongest self-concept.

Fourth, they narrow responsibility to one job. Not ten. Not everything. One clear action. The brain performs best when responsibility is singular. This tactical simplification prevents cognitive overload and channels all available mental resources toward the most important immediate action.

These are not motivational tricks.

They are neurological controls.

Chaos Is Neutral—You Assign Meaning

Chaos offers two interpretations. Either this moment is too big for me or this moment was built for me. The moment does not decide that—you do. This fundamental choice determines whether pressure becomes debilitating or energizing, whether challenges appear as threats or opportunities.

Chaos can represent danger or destiny. Pressure can be perceived as risk or proof. The objective circumstances remain identical—only the interpretation changes. Yet this interpretation completely transforms our access to capabilities, creativity, and confidence under fire.

Elite performers do not wait for chaos to disappear. They operate inside it without losing identity. This capacity to maintain core principles, values, and self-concept during turbulence becomes a defining characteristic of high-performing individuals, teams, and organizations. For the Missionpreneur, this skill translates directly into resilience during market shifts, competitive challenges, and strategic pivots.

Why Slowing Down Wins Fights

When the world spins faster, amateurs speed up emotionally. Warriors slow down internally. This counterintuitive response pattern distinguishes elite performers across domains—from combat pilots to emergency surgeons to crisis negotiators to championship athletes. The capacity to decelerate internally as external pressure intensifies represents a master-level performance skill.

Anyone can react. Anyone can panic. Anyone can get loud or erratic. These default responses require no training or discipline—they emerge automatically from our survival programming when faced with threat or pressure.

Slow is powerful. In moments of chaos, the person who maintains internal composure gains immediate advantages in perception, decision-making, and execution. This controlled response creates a decisive edge in high-stakes situations.

When the mind slows, emotions stabilize. When emotions stabilize, clarity rises. When clarity rises, execution becomes automatic. This virtuous cascade enables peak performance precisely when stakes are highest and pressure is most intense.

Slowing down is not weakness.

It is control.

The Clarity Formula

Whenever chaos begins to overwhelm, the response must be automatic. This operational protocol should be practiced until it becomes an unconscious sequence that activates immediately under pressure. For Missionpreneurs facing complex decisions and high-stakes moments, this formula provides a reliable path back to optimal performance.

First, breathe to regulate the body.

Second, anchor identity with a simple truth.

Third, narrow focus to one job.

Fourth, attack the moment—not the outcome.

You do not need the situation to calm down.

You need yourself to calm down.

Focus as a Transferable Leadership Skill

Focus under fire is not just a performance tool—it is a leadership multiplier. Teams take emotional cues from leaders. Families watch how leaders respond under stress. Organizations mirror the clarity—or chaos—of those in charge. This emotional contagion effect means that a leader's mental state becomes magnified throughout their sphere of influence.

Leaders who panic spread panic.

Leaders who remain clear spread confidence.

Focus is contagious. When a leader maintains composure during crisis, it creates a psychologically safe environment where teams can access their best capabilities rather than defaulting to survival reactions. This emotional leadership directly impacts decision quality, communication effectiveness, and execution precision during high-pressure situations.

Training Focus Before It's Needed

You cannot develop focus under fire during the fire. It must be trained in advance. This preparation principle applies to all high-performance domains—from emergency response to military operations to business leadership. The capabilities that emerge under extreme pressure reflect the quality and consistency of prior preparation.

This happens through intentional discomfort, simulated pressure, deliberate practice, reflection after failure, controlled adversity, and disciplined identity work. These training modalities systematically strengthen the neural pathways and psychological patterns that sustain clarity during chaos. For Missionpreneurs, this means creating intentional practice opportunities that build focus resilience before major challenges arise.

Pressure does not reward potential.

Pressure rewards preparation.

Why Focus Is the Hidden Divider

Talent is common. Effort is common. Ambition is common. Focus under chaos is rare. This scarcity creates extraordinary competitive advantage for those who develop this capability. In markets flooded with comparable products, services, and capabilities, the ability to maintain clarity during disruption becomes a decisive differentiator.

That is why so few people perform consistently when stakes are high. The very conditions that demand our best performance tend to trigger psychological and physiological responses that impair access to our capabilities. This paradox explains why potential so often goes unrealized in crucial moments.

Focus is not charisma.

It is control.

And control under pressure separates elite from average. For the Missionpreneur building a legacy, this capacity to maintain clarity amidst chaos becomes a defining characteristic that shapes not just performance outcomes but leadership impact.

Reflection Questions

1. What conditions cause your focus to collapse most quickly—pressure, fatigue, emotion, mistakes, or expectations?
2. When chaos hits, where does your mind drift—past, future, or present?
3. What identity phrase can serve as your mental anchor under pressure?
4. What habit or environment would help you train focus under fire rather than hoping pressure disappears?
5. What is the single job you must lock into during your next high-stakes moment?

Closing Declaration

Chaos does not control me.

Confusion does not lead me.

Pressure does not define me.

I remain clear when the world is loud.

I stay present when outcomes are heavy.

I execute when others overreact.

I do not wait for calm.

I create clarity.

I am a Missionpreneur, and I focus under fire.

CHAPTER 14

RAISING BUILDERS, NOT BENEFICIARIES

Why Legacy Is Multiplied Through Preparation, Not Provision

Every generation answers one defining question—either by design or by default: Will what was built be multiplied... or merely spent? This question shapes the trajectory of family businesses, wealth transfers, and value systems across generations. The answer determines whether your legacy becomes a launchpad or a landing pad for those who follow.

Legacy does not usually disappear in one dramatic failure. It erodes quietly through unprepared successors who lack the capacity, character, and conviction to steward what they've received. When provision outpaces preparation, inheritance becomes a burden instead of a blessing. The transfer of resources without the transfer of responsibility creates an imbalance that few legacies survive.

The danger is not wealth, access, or opportunity.

The danger is inheritance given to people who were never trained to steward it.

Missionpreneurs understand this truth early and implement systems to address it proactively. They do not confuse blessing with indulgence or mistake comfort for care. They recognize that the goal is not to raise children who benefit from legacy—but children who are capable of bearing it. This distinction shapes every decision about family governance, resource allocation, and leadership development.

The Entitlement Trap

Entitlement is rarely intentional. It is not rebellion or defiance—it is expectation without responsibility. It forms gradually, almost imperceptibly, when children receive access without accountability, inherit benefits without understanding cost, and are protected from failure instead of trained through it. Most entitlement is born from love misapplied, not laziness or malice.

Parents want to bless.

But blessing without building produces fragility.

What you give without training weakens what you hope to preserve. What you provide without formation quietly erodes gratitude, humility, and responsibility. Entitlement does not announce itself loudly with obvious warning signs. It whispers expectations, resists correction, and manifests in subtle attitudes rather than overt demands. The entitled heir rarely recognizes their condition until confronted with responsibility they cannot handle.

Left unchecked, it kills legacy from the inside, hollowing out the very foundations that made success possible in the first place. Family businesses, wealth, and influence collapse not from external threats but from internal weakness.

Why Beneficiaries Destroy Legacy

Beneficiaries consume systems.

Builders strengthen them.

A beneficiary mindset seeks reward without contribution, access without ownership, and position without proof. It avoids responsibility, deflects accountability, and resists correction. It sees inheritance as entitlement rather than trust, viewing legacy as something owed rather than something entrusted. This perspective treats resources as rights rather than responsibilities.

A builder mindset values process over privilege, understands cost, accepts responsibility, and honors stewardship. Builders approach legacy with a fundamentally different question. Builders ask, What is required of me? Beneficiaries ask, What am I owed? This distinction in mindset determines whether resources become fuel for growth or fodder for decline.

Legacy does not survive on comfort.

It survives on competence and conviction.

Every enduring legacy in Scripture, business, and history was carried forward by builders—not beneficiaries. From the biblical patriarchs to multi-generational family enterprises, the pattern remains consistent: legacy thrives when the next generation builds upon what they receive rather than merely consuming it.

The Missionpreneur Parenting Distinction

Missionpreneurs do not raise dependents.

They raise stewards.

Stewardship is not inherited. It is trained through intentional processes that develop capacity alongside character. It develops through responsibility that is real, not symbolic; correction that is consistent, not sporadic; consequences that are appropriate, not absent; and accountability that is loving but firm. Protection has its place in parenting—but protection that prevents growth produces fragility rather than strength.

Missionpreneur parents understand that their role is not to eliminate discomfort, but to prepare capacity. Children must learn to carry weight before they inherit influence. This preparation begins early, increases gradually, and continues consistently. The development of stewardship follows a progressive path where responsibility increases in proportion to demonstrated capacity.

Work as Formation, Not Punishment

Modern culture treats work as something to avoid—a necessary evil to be minimized. Scripture treats work as something that forms—a divine tool for character development. This fundamental difference in perspective shapes how we introduce children to responsibility and contribution.

Work teaches discipline, ownership, humility, perseverance, and delayed gratification. It reveals strengths and exposes weaknesses in ways that theoretical instruction cannot. It builds competence and character simultaneously, creating a foundation for leadership that cannot be established through privilege alone. Work connects effort to outcomes in ways that shape a realistic worldview.

Missionpreneur families assign work not as punishment, but as preparation. Chores, responsibilities, and contribution are not beneath children—they are for children. If children never experience contribution, they never understand value. If they never participate in the work that generates resources, they cannot properly steward those resources. This disconnection between effort and outcome creates a distorted view of reality.

Work teaches a critical lesson: results are connected to effort. That lesson protects legacy far more than money ever could. When children understand this connection early, they develop both capability and appreciation. They learn to value what they help create and protect what they help build.

Biblical Example: David and Solomon—Two Approaches to Preparation

David prepared Solomon extensively for leadership and kingdom stewardship. He did not just pass on resources—he passed on plans, systems, values, instruction, and accountability. Solomon inherited wealth, but he also inherited structure. This preparation included specific instructions, dedicated resources, identified partners, and clear expectations—a comprehensive leadership transition plan rather than merely a transfer of assets.

Even with preparation, Solomon's later drift shows how fragile legacy can be without ongoing stewardship. Despite his wisdom and preparation, Solomon eventually compromised the very values that established his kingdom. Scripture reminds us that inheritance alone does not guarantee obedience. Initial preparation must be followed by continual recommitment to founding principles.

This underscores a central truth: preparation must outpace provision, and formation must continue long after access begins. Legacy transfer is not a single event but an ongoing process that requires vigilance, accountability, and renewal. Each generation must reestablish commitment to founding values while adapting implementation to current realities.

The Apprenticeship Pathway

Inheritance is not transferred in a moment. It is built through stages that develop capacity progressively. Skipping these stages creates leaders who appear qualified but lack foundational strength.

First comes observation. Children watch how decisions are made, how conflict is handled, how money is managed, how authority is respected, and how failure is processed. What you model silently shapes them more than anything you say. This observational learning creates mental frameworks that guide future behavior and establishes patterns that persist long after formal instruction ends.

Then comes participation. Children serve alongside you in appropriate capacities. They help, they try, and they fail in controlled environments where learning is prioritized. Mistakes are expected. Correction is normal. Learning accelerates through guided experience rather than theoretical instruction. Participation builds confidence alongside competence.

Next comes ownership. Responsibility becomes real rather than symbolic. Outcomes matter. Accountability increases. Excuses are removed. Children take complete responsibility for defined areas, experiencing both the rewards of success and the consequences of failure. This ownership stage reveals character and develops judgment in ways that participation cannot.

Finally comes leadership. They lead independently, but not without boundaries. Authority expands with demonstrated stewardship. They begin to direct others, manage resources, and make significant decisions. This leadership stage tests both competence and character under pressure, revealing readiness for greater responsibility.

Skipping stages produces fragile leaders who look confident but collapse under responsibility. They possess position without preparation, authority without accountability, and influence without internal strength. Legacy requires leaders who have developed through each stage, not those who were merely appointed to leadership.

Why Failure Is Non-Negotiable

Failure is not the enemy.

Uncorrected failure is.

Missionpreneurs allow appropriate failure within safe boundaries. They permit real consequences and give honest feedback without rescuing prematurely. Failure handled well builds resilience, judgment, and humility—essential qualities for long-term leadership. Failure avoided entirely builds fear, entitlement, and fragility—qualities that undermine legacy preservation.

Children who never fail never develop discernment. They learn to avoid risk rather than manage responsibility. They become paralyzed by perfectionism or reckless from inexperience. Neither extreme serves legacy well. Legacy requires people who can recover, not people who panic. It needs leaders who learn from mistakes rather than those who never make them or never acknowledge them.

Failure is part of training, not evidence of disqualification. It reveals character, exposes weaknesses, and creates opportunity for growth that cannot be achieved through success alone. The question is not whether failure will occur, but how it will be processed. Will it become a learning opportunity or a source of shame? Will it build resilience or reinforce fear?

Separating Love from Entitlement

Love provides.

Entitlement assumes.

Missionpreneurs teach that access is earned, leadership is proven, and resources follow stewardship. This does not diminish love. It protects dignity and develops capacity. When children understand that privileges are connected to responsibility, they develop both appreciation and capability. When they believe everything is owed to them, they develop neither.

People value what they work for. They often squander what they are handed without effort or appreciation. Entitlement is not kind—it is corrosive to both character and capacity. Stewardship builds respect for both people and provision. It creates a healthy relationship with resources rather than a dependent one.

True love prepares children for reality rather than protecting them from it. It equips them to thrive independently rather than depending perpetually. Missionpreneurs demonstrate love through preparation, not just provision. They invest in capacity building alongside resource sharing.

The Hidden Danger of Over-Provision

Over-provision often masquerades as generosity. It appears loving, supportive, and well-intentioned. But when provision eliminates effort, initiative declines, gratitude fades, and responsibility erodes. Excessive provision creates a false reality that cannot be sustained and develops expectations that cannot be fulfilled.

Provision should support growth—not replace it. It should enhance capacity rather than substituting for it. The question is not whether to provide, but how to provide in ways that strengthen rather than weaken. Timing, amount, and conditions matter as much as the provision itself.

Missionpreneurs are intentional about how they provide, not just what they provide. They ask whether assistance develops capacity or delays maturity. They consider whether support enables growth or encourages dependence. Over-provision weakens muscles that were meant to grow. It creates artificial environments that do not prepare children for the realities they must eventually face.

Builders Understand Cost

True builders understand that sacrifice precedes reward, discipline precedes freedom, and responsibility precedes authority. This understanding of sequence and causality shapes their approach to both leadership and life. They recognize that bypassing these sequences creates weakness rather than advantage.

Missionpreneurs do not shield children from cost. They teach them to count it accurately and accept it willingly. Counting cost prepares children for leadership in a world where resources are limited and trade-offs are required. Avoiding cost prepares them for dependence in a fantasy where everything is available without sacrifice. Reality eventually reveals which preparation was authentic.

Legacy cannot be carried by people who expect ease. The weight of responsibility requires strength that comes only through resistance and challenge. Those who have never experienced difficulty cannot manage complexity. Those who have never sacrificed cannot appreciate value. Those who have never persevered cannot sustain commitment when obstacles arise.

The Builder's Metric

Here is a simple test of readiness for greater responsibility and leadership within your legacy: If resources were removed, would competence remain? This question cuts through appearance to reveal reality.

If money, access, and influence disappeared, would skills, discipline, and character still be present? Would the capacity to rebuild exist independent of current position? If not, preparation is incomplete and additional development is required. This assessment reveals the difference between those who appear successful and those who are truly capable.

Legacy is not secure until competence exists independent of comfort. Position that depends on privilege rather than capability cannot withstand challenge. Leadership that relies on title rather than skill cannot adapt to changing circumstances. Influence that stems from inheritance rather than impact cannot survive scrutiny.

Builder Formation Audit

Every Missionpreneur parent must periodically ask hard questions about the development of the next generation. These questions reveal gaps in preparation that might otherwise remain hidden until crisis exposes them.

Do my children understand how resources are generated, or do they simply expect provision? Have they experienced real responsibility with consequences, or only symbolic tasks without accountability? Are expectations clear or assumed? Is leadership earned or automatic? Is correction consistent or emotional? Do they understand the difference between ownership and access?

Every "no" reveals where entitlement could quietly form and where preparation remains incomplete. These gaps represent vulnerabilities in your legacy transition plan that must be addressed proactively rather than reactively. Identifying them early allows for developmental interventions before patterns become entrenched.

Correction Builds Character

Correction is not punishment. It is direction that guides development and shapes character. When delivered appropriately, correction communicates care rather than criticism. It establishes boundaries that protect rather than restrict.

Avoiding correction to preserve peace builds weakness, not relationship. It prioritizes temporary comfort over lasting development. Missionpreneur parents correct early, clearly, lovingly, and consistently. They separate discipline from emotion and instruction from anger. They ensure correction addresses behavior without attacking identity.

Correction communicates belief. It says, You are capable of growth, and I expect more from you. It establishes standards that stretch capacity rather than accommodating comfort. It refuses to accept less than what is possible while providing support for development.

That message builds confidence, not resentment. Children internalize the belief that they are capable of meeting high standards rather than requiring lowered expectations. They develop internal discipline rather than external compliance. They learn to evaluate their own performance rather than depending on others for assessment.

Why Builders Protect Legacy Better Than Rules

Rules control behavior temporarily. Builders govern themselves through internalized principles that transcend specific situations. Rules require enforcement; principles provide guidance.

Rules address actions; principles shape decisions. Rules operate externally; principles function internally.

Missionpreneurs are not raising rule-followers. They are raising principle-driven leaders who understand the "why" behind the "what." Builders make wise decisions even when no one is watching because they operate from conviction rather than compliance. Beneficiaries comply only when supervised because they lack internal governance.

Legacy survives when internal discipline replaces external enforcement. This transition from external control to internal governance represents the true transfer of values across generations. Without this transition, legacy requires constant supervision that becomes impossible at scale or over time.

Generational Strength Is the Goal

The goal of legacy is not comfort for the next generation. It is strength. Strength of character, clarity of identity, discipline of habits, and courage of conviction. These qualities enable the next generation to both preserve and expand what they receive rather than merely maintaining it.

Every generation must be stronger than the last, or decline is inevitable. Each generation faces new challenges that require new capabilities. Maintaining previous standards is insufficient; capacity must increase to meet escalating complexity. Missionpreneurs understand that love without formation is not kindness—it is negligence that leaves the next generation unprepared for the responsibilities they will inherit.

Reflection Questions

1. Where might my provision be outpacing preparation in my family or business? What specific areas show signs of access without corresponding responsibility?

2. What responsibilities should my children be carrying that I've been protecting them from? Which tasks am I completing that they should be learning to manage?

3. How do I currently respond to my children's failure—rescue or refinement? Do I intervene too quickly or allow appropriate consequences to teach valuable lessons?

4. What specific skill,

Closing Declaration

Legacy does not survive on inheritance alone.

It survives when the next generation is stronger, wiser, and more disciplined than the one before.

I refuse to raise beneficiaries who protect comfort.

I commit to raise builders who carry responsibility.

What I build must be something my children can steward—not something that corrupts them.

I am a Missionpreneur, and I raise builders—not beneficiaries.

CHAPTER 15

ENTERPRISE WITH ETERNAL INTENT

Building Organizations That Outlive You and Outlast Trends

Enterprise is never neutral. It either amplifies purpose—or accelerates drift. Every organizational decision either reinforces mission or subtly erodes it, creating either alignment or confusion. The impact of these choices compounds over time, shaping not just quarterly results but generational outcomes.

Every organization—business, ministry, institution, nonprofit, school, or brand—becomes a megaphone for the values of its leaders. What you build speaks long after you stop talking. The structures you create, the policies you implement, and the culture you foster continue communicating your priorities even when you're no longer present. This organizational echo extends far beyond your tenure.

Missionpreneurs do not ask only, Will this work? They ask, What will this shape over time? This deeper questioning transforms decision-making from transactional to transformational. Rather than evaluating choices solely on efficiency or profitability metrics, missionpreneurs examine how each decision shapes character, reinforces values, and influences stakeholders.

Because enterprise is not just about what it produces. It is about what it produces in people. The products, services, and profits generated by any organization represent only its surface-level output. The deeper impact—and ultimately more significant legacy—lies in how the enterprise forms the character, capabilities, and convictions of everyone it touches.

Whether intentionally or unintentionally, every organization trains its people. It disciples habits, attitudes, ethics, expectations, and decision-making frameworks. Neutrality is an illusion. Silence still teaches. Systems still preach. When leaders fail to deliberately shape culture, culture shapes itself—often in ways that undermine stated values and long-term sustainability. The absence of intentional formation doesn't prevent formation; it simply surrenders it to default patterns.

The Myth of "Just Business"

Modern culture separates faith and enterprise as if they belong in different categories. Business is framed as practical rather than spiritual, neutral rather than formative, results-driven rather than values-driven. This artificial compartmentalization creates a dangerous disconnect between stated beliefs and operational realities. It enables leaders to profess one set of values while building systems that reward their opposite.

Scripture dismantles that myth. Throughout biblical narrative, economic activity is never portrayed as morally neutral or spiritually insignificant. From the Garden of Eden to the New Jerusalem, work, commerce, and resource management are consistently presented as deeply spiritual activities with profound ethical implications. The biblical worldview offers no separate category for "just business" decisions detached from moral considerations.

Work existed before the fall. Stewardship was assigned before sin entered the world. Enterprise was part of God's design before corruption ever touched it. Business did not become broken because it was created—it became broken because it was detached from intent. This historical perspective reclaims the inherent dignity and purpose of commerce as part of creation's original design, not a necessary evil or morally neutral activity.

Enterprise is not unspiritual. It is deeply formative. Every aspect of organizational life—from hiring practices to customer interactions, from compensation structures to conflict resolution processes—shapes human hearts and minds. When we recognize this formative power, we approach business decisions with appropriate reverence and responsibility.

What you build shapes hearts, habits, hierarchies, and human potential. Your enterprise molds how people perceive authority, handle resources, resolve conflicts, and pursue excellence. It influences their understanding of success, their approach to relationships, and their sense of purpose. This formative impact extends far beyond working hours, affecting families, communities, and future generations.

Why Success Without Intent Is Dangerous

Organizations can grow faster than character when intent is unclear. Without eternal intent, profit replaces purpose, speed replaces discernment, and expansion replaces obedience. The organization may thrive financially while hollowing out morally, relationally, and spiritually. This internal erosion often remains invisible until crisis reveals the structural weakness beneath apparent success.

Missionpreneurs understand that growth without grounding leads to collapse. History is littered with enterprises that scaled quickly and crumbled suddenly—not because the idea was bad, but because formation was absent. When organizations prioritize expansion over alignment, efficiency over integrity, or market share over mission clarity, they create the conditions for eventual implosion. The very success that seems impressive becomes unsustainable.

Intent is what stabilizes scale. Clear, consistent, and communicated purpose provides the foundation that supports healthy growth. Without this anchoring intent, expansion creates complexity that overwhelms systems, dilutes culture, and fragments leadership. With intent firmly established, however, the same growth strengthens rather than weakens the organization, creating sustainable momentum and increasing impact.

Eternal Intent Clarified

Eternal intent does not mean ignoring profit, rejecting excellence, or avoiding competition. It means profit serves mission, excellence reflects stewardship, and competition sharpens without compromise. This clarification prevents the false dichotomy that forces leaders to choose between financial sustainability and faithful mission. Properly understood, eternal intent integrates economic viability with eternal values.

Eternal intent answers one essential question: Who is this enterprise forming? This question shifts focus from what the organization produces to who it shapes. It examines not just operational outputs but formational outcomes. By prioritizing formation, missionpreneurs create enterprises that generate both economic and eternal returns—organizations that produce both profits and people of character.

Employees are being shaped. Leaders are being trained. Customers are being influenced. Families are being affected by the policies, pressures, and priorities of the organization. Every stakeholder interaction represents a formational moment—an opportunity to reinforce values, demonstrate character, and develop capacity. These countless micro-interactions collectively determine whether the organization's impact strengthens or undermines its stated mission.

Missionpreneurs refuse to outsource formation to chance. They recognize that character development is too important to occur accidentally. Instead, they deliberately design systems, structures, and experiences that cultivate desired qualities and capabilities. They create intentional pathways for growth, clear frameworks for decision-making, and consistent accountability for alignment. Formation becomes a strategic priority rather than a hoped-for byproduct.

Business as a Discipleship Platform

Enterprise is one of the most powerful discipleship platforms in the modern world. People spend more waking hours inside organizations than almost anywhere else. They learn what is rewarded, what is tolerated, and what is required by watching leaders—not mission statements. This reality makes the workplace a primary arena for character formation, whether intentionally leveraged or not.

Policies preach. Systems teach. Behavior modeled becomes belief adopted. The operational mechanics of an organization communicate values more powerfully than any written document or verbal declaration. How meetings are conducted, how decisions are made, how conflicts are resolved, and how success is measured—these daily realities shape convictions and character more profoundly than formal training programs.

What leaders tolerate eventually becomes culture. What leaders confront becomes alignment. This principle applies to both positive and negative behaviors. When excellence goes unrecognized, mediocrity becomes acceptable. When ethical compromises go unchallenged, integrity erodes. Conversely, when leaders consistently reinforce values through recognition and correction, those values become embedded in organizational DNA.

Missionpreneurs leverage enterprise as a training ground for leaders, a laboratory for character, and a proving field for stewardship. They do not merely extract value from people—they invest value into them. This developmental approach transforms the organization from a mere production mechanism into a formation community. Work becomes not just a means of earning but an environment for learning, growing, and maturing in capability and character.

Biblical Example: Joseph — Enterprise with Eternal Intent

Joseph's leadership in Egypt provides one of the clearest pictures of enterprise governed by eternal intent. He operated at the highest economic levels of his time, managing resources, planning infrastructure, and executing large-scale systems. His responsibilities included forecasting, logistics, inventory management, distribution networks, and crisis response—all core business functions that required exceptional administrative skill.

Yet Joseph never detached success from stewardship. He did not use power for ego or wealth for self-preservation. He used enterprise to save lives, stabilize a nation, and preserve God's redemptive plan. His economic leadership remained connected to eternal purpose. He recognized his position as an assignment rather than an achievement, maintaining humility despite unprecedented authority.

Joseph proves that economic authority and spiritual authority are not opposites when intent is aligned. His story demolishes the false dichotomy between marketplace success and kingdom impact. Joseph demonstrates that organizational excellence, economic wisdom, and eternal purpose can coexist and reinforce each other. His legacy challenges modern missionpreneurs to reject compartmentalization and pursue integration of faith and enterprise.

The Missionpreneur ROI

The world defines return on investment through profit, growth, and speed. Missionpreneurs use a broader ledger. While they recognize the importance of financial sustainability, they measure success through multiple dimensions that capture both immediate outcomes and long-term impact. This expanded definition of ROI creates enterprises that generate returns beyond quarterly statements.

They ask: Who was developed? Who was strengthened? Who matured in responsibility, clarity, and conviction? Who is now capable of leading others? These human development metrics reveal whether the organization is creating lasting value or merely extracting temporary gain. By tracking formation outcomes alongside financial ones, missionpreneurs ensure the enterprise builds both economic and eternal equity.

Financial profit is necessary. Human profit is essential. Without financial sustainability, an organization cannot continue its mission. Without human development, that mission becomes hollow regardless of financial success. Missionpreneurs pursue both, recognizing that truly successful enterprises generate multiple forms of capital—financial, intellectual, relational, and spiritual.

An enterprise that grows revenue but shrinks people is consuming itself. It creates the illusion of progress while depleting its most valuable resource—the character, capability, and commitment of its people. This self-cannibalizing growth eventually collapses as burnout, turnover, and cultural erosion undermine the foundation. Sustainable enterprises develop people while delivering profits, creating reinforcing cycles of growth rather than extractive ones.

When Opportunity Outruns Assignment

Some of the most damaging decisions are good ones. Expansion looks attractive. Partnerships seem logical. Funding arrives easily. These opportunities often appear beneficial on the surface, presenting compelling financial projections, market advantages, or growth potential. Their apparent merit makes them particularly dangerous when they subtly shift the organization away from its core assignment.

Missionpreneurs understand a sobering truth: opportunity is not assignment. Open doors still require discernment. Not every door opened by man was opened by God. This discernment requires both courage and clarity—courage to decline attractive opportunities that would create mission drift, and clarity about the specific assignment that defines the organization's purpose and boundaries.

Speed without assignment creates chaos. Growth without obedience creates drift. When organizations pursue opportunities faster than they can integrate them into their mission and culture, they create internal fragmentation. Systems strain, communication breaks down, and values become diluted. What begins as exciting expansion often ends as exhausting complexity that undermines the very mission it was meant to advance.

Eternal enterprises move deliberately—even when momentum invites haste. They maintain disciplined alignment between opportunity and assignment, evaluating potential growth not just by its financial or strategic merit but by its formational impact. This deliberate approach may sometimes appear slower than market-driven alternatives, but it creates sustainable momentum rather than temporary acceleration followed by corrective retreats.

The Eternal Enterprise Filter

Before growth decisions, Missionpreneurs slow down long enough to ask difficult questions. They create intentional pauses in the decision process to ensure alignment between opportunity and assignment. These reflection points serve as protective filters, screening out attractive options that would ultimately undermine mission integrity or organizational health.

Does this expansion align with our mission or dilute it? Who will this shape, and in what direction? Are we stewarding authority—or striving for relevance? Can this endure without compromising values? Does this strengthen leadership pipelines—or centralize power further? These questions examine both the immediate impact and long-term implications of potential decisions, preventing short-term thinking that creates long-term problems.

Growth that undermines formation is not progress. It is acceleration toward dysfunction. When expansion outpaces character development, weakens cultural cohesion, or compromises core values, it creates organizational debt that eventually comes due—often at the most inopportune moments. True progress strengthens rather than strains the organization's identity, capacity, and sustainability.

Systems Reveal Values

Missionpreneurs do not measure values by what is written on walls, but by what is rewarded in systems. They recognize that operational reality trumps aspirational rhetoric every time. When examining organizational values, they look beyond mission statements and corporate declarations to the actual mechanisms that drive daily decisions and determine outcomes.

Who gets promoted—and why? How is conflict handled? What behavior is corrected—and what is ignored? Where is pressure applied—and where is grace extended? These system-level questions reveal the true priorities of the organization more accurately than any published values list. The answers expose whether stated values have been operationalized or merely idealized.

Systems never lie. If systems contradict stated values, values are aspirational rather than operational. When compensation structures reward individual achievement while leadership claims to value collaboration, the system reveals the truth. When advancement requires sacrificing family while the organization professes work-life balance, the contradiction exposes the actual priorities at work.

Eternal intent must be embedded structurally—not merely declared verbally. Missionpreneurs align systems with values, ensuring that operational mechanisms reinforce rather than undermine stated priorities. They design hiring processes, performance reviews, compensation structures, and advancement pathways that consistently reward and reinforce the behaviors and outcomes they claim to value.

Enterprise Without Discipleship Creates Mercenaries

When people are used to build organizations but are not built within them, loyalty erodes. Turnover increases. Culture fragments. People become transactional rather than committed. This pattern occurs predictably in organizations that prioritize production over formation, treating people as interchangeable resources rather than developing them as irreplaceable assets.

Missionpreneurs refuse to treat people as tools. Teams are not resources to be consumed—they are trainees being formed. This developmental mindset transforms the employment relationship from extraction to investment. Rather than merely using people's skills to achieve organizational objectives, missionpreneurs deliberately develop capabilities, character, and conviction through intentional training, meaningful feedback, and progressive responsibility.

Discipleship builds ownership. Ownership builds loyalty. Loyalty stabilizes legacy. When people experience genuine development within an organization, they develop psychological ownership that transcends transactional engagement. This ownership creates loyalty that withstands challenges, sustains momentum through transitions, and preserves mission continuity across generations.

Excellence as Worship

Missionpreneurs pursue excellence not to impress—but to honor stewardship. Sloppy systems dishonor the people they affect. Confusion creates frustration. Inconsistency breeds distrust. Excellence in execution demonstrates respect for both the mission and the people it serves, reflecting the conviction that how something is done matters as much as what is accomplished.

Excellence is not perfectionism. It is faithfulness executed well. It communicates care, respect, and responsibility. Unlike perfectionism, which stems from fear and creates paralysis, true excellence flows from stewardship and creates momentum. It sets high standards without creating crushing expectations, pushing teams toward their best without breaking their spirit.

God deserves our best. People deserve clarity. Legacy requires durability. These three principles establish excellence as a moral imperative rather than a marketing advantage. Excellence honors God as the ultimate owner of all resources, respects people as inherently valuable, and builds organizations capable of sustaining impact beyond the current leadership generation.

The Hidden Risk of Centralized Knowledge

Most enterprises fail during transition, not expansion. Why? Because knowledge is centralized, authority is unclear, and culture depends on the founder's personality. These vulnerabilities often remain hidden during periods of stability but emerge catastrophically during leadership transitions. Organizations built around individuals rather than intentional systems struggle to survive their founders.

Missionpreneurs refuse to build personality-dependent organizations. They document systems, distribute authority, train successors, and embed intent into structure. This deliberate decentralization creates organizational resilience that withstands leadership transitions. Knowledge becomes institutional rather than individual, preserved in processes and training rather than residing exclusively in founding leaders' minds.

An enterprise with eternal intent does not panic when leadership changes—because values do not change with faces. The organization's identity, direction, and operational excellence remain consistent despite personnel transitions because they've been systematically embedded rather than personally embodied. This continuity provides stability for stakeholders and sustainability for the mission.

Succession Is a Spiritual Responsibility

Succession planning transcends mere operational strategy—it represents a profound moral responsibility for values-driven leaders. When properly executed, succession ensures organizational continuity and preserves the mission's integrity through leadership transitions. However, when leadership transfer creates organizational chaos, confusion, or operational collapse, the fundamental issue isn't timing—it's inadequate preparation and intentional development.

Authentic missionpreneurs build robust leadership pipelines long before they are needed, recognizing that effective succession requires years of deliberate mentoring and character formation. They create systems where emerging leaders can develop decision-making capabilities while still under guidance. The most resilient organizations normalize leadership transitions through transparent processes that honor institutional wisdom while embracing fresh perspectives.

Legacy truly survives when leadership transition is expected, systematically trained for, and culturally normalized throughout the organization. This preparation demonstrates stewardship that extends beyond quarterly results to generational impact.

Enterprise as a Witness

Whether leaders explicitly acknowledge it or not, every enterprise bears witness to its underlying values through daily operations and decisions. Customers, employees, and communities form lasting impressions about faith, leadership principles, and organizational integrity based on observable patterns—how the organization treats people during challenges, handles failure with accountability, honors commitments despite inconvenience, and operates under financial or market pressure.

Discerning missionpreneurs understand that enterprise built with eternal intent naturally becomes a powerful testimony—even without explicit preaching or promotional messaging. They recognize that operational integrity speaks volumes about organizational values in ways that mission statements alone cannot. When stated principles align with operational practices, the organization's witness gains authentic credibility in the marketplace.

Integrity consistently demonstrated through business practices resonates far more powerfully than beliefs merely stated in corporate documents. This lived testimony creates a distinctive organizational character that stakeholders recognize and respect, even when they don't share identical values.

Why Eternal Intent Outlasts Trends

In today's business landscape, markets change with increasing velocity, technologies shift unpredictably, leaders inevitably age and transition, organizational seasons naturally end, and market trends expire with alarming speed. These external factors create tremendous pressure for reactive decision-making that can compromise long-term organizational identity.

However, intent embedded deeply within organizational DNA does not succumb to these pressures. Purpose-driven enterprises built with eternal perspective maintain their essential character while adapting to changing circumstances. This foundational intent creates resilient organizations that successfully adapt without abandoning core identity, evolve methodologies without eroding fundamental values, and remain culturally relevant without becoming ethically reckless.

Organizational durability—the capacity to weather economic cycles, leadership transitions, and market disruptions while maintaining mission alignment—stands as the definitive mark of faithful enterprise. This durability doesn't guarantee permanent market dominance, but it does ensure that the organization's impact remains consistent with its founding purpose through inevitable changes.

Reflection Questions for Missionpreneurs

1. What specific values is my enterprise currently forming in stakeholders—both intentionally through stated principles and unintentionally through operational patterns?

2. In which areas of our organization might rapid growth be outrunning character formation and leadership development?

3. Do our operational systems, compensation structures, and decision-making processes genuinely reinforce our stated mission—or subtly contradict it through misaligned incentives?

4. How is leadership being systematically multiplied throughout the organization—not just productive output or revenue generation?

5. Would this organization still clearly reflect eternal intent and foundational values if I were suddenly absent from leadership?

6. What specific processes have we implemented to ensure values transmission during growth phases and leadership transitions?

Closing Declaration

I categorically refuse to build something that appears impressive externally but remains hollow in substance and purpose.

I commit instead to build something genuinely formative for stakeholders and faithful to foundational values.

In my enterprise, profit will consistently serve purpose—not dictate it.

Operational systems will transparently reflect stated values—not undermine them.

People will be intentionally built and developed—not merely used as resources.

My enterprise will methodically train leaders at every level, strengthen character through consistent practices, and outlast short-term market trends through principled adaptation.

Organizational success will never come at the cost of obedience to foundational calling and values.

I am a Missionpreneur, and I build with eternal intent that transcends quarterly metrics and shapes generational impact.

CHAPTER 16

BUILDING A LIFE THAT WON'T BREAK YOU

Systems, Values, and Structure for Sustainable High Performance

It's one thing to win. It's another thing entirely to win without losing yourself in the process. The distinction between these two outcomes represents the difference between momentary achievement and lasting legacy.

Many people achieve success—then collapse under the weight of that success. Not because they lacked talent or ambition, but because their life was never built to sustain the level of greatness they were chasing. Their foundation was too fragile for the structure they erected upon it.

High performance is not just about how big you can build. It's about how much you can build without breaking. This sustainability factor often separates those who make history from those who become cautionary tales.

Talent, passion, hunger, discipline, drive, and work ethic can take you far. But without structure, those same qualities can take you straight into burnout, emotional exhaustion, relational damage, and identity collapse. Your greatest strengths, without proper channels, can become the forces that destroy you.

You don't need a life that can produce big moments. You need a life that can support a lifetime of big moments. The architecture of sustainable success is what we'll explore in this chapter—how to build a life that amplifies your impact without diminishing your wholeness.

Why So Many Strong People Break

Most breakdowns don't happen because someone is weak. They happen because someone is overextended without support. Success amplifies everything—strengths and fractures alike. When pressure increases, whatever cracks exist will widen until the structure fails.

Winning doesn't heal insecurity; it multiplies it. Winning doesn't fix weak discipline; it exposes it. Winning doesn't eliminate fear; it magnifies it. The spotlight of success reveals everything you've been hiding, even from yourself.

That's why the most dangerous lie ambitious people believe is: "I'll slow down after I succeed." This deception has led countless high-achievers down a path of irreversible damage to their health, relationships, and inner peace.

You don't build your foundation after success arrives. You build it before—or you pay for it later. This principle applies whether you're building a business, a ministry, a platform, or any endeavor of significance. The infrastructure must precede the weight it will carry.

The Three Levels of Winning

There are three types of winners in life, each with distinct trajectories and outcomes. Understanding these archetypes helps us choose our path intentionally rather than defaulting to cultural expectations.

Some win fast and burn out even faster. Their success is loud but short-lived. They rise quickly and implode quietly. The meteoric rise makes headlines; the subsequent fall happens behind closed doors. These are the cautionary tales we rarely learn from until we become one.

Some win through relentless sacrifice. They grind, endure, and persevere—but the cost is brutal. Health erodes. Relationships fracture. Peace disappears. They win, but everything else loses. Their trophies sit on empty shelves in empty homes.

Then there are sustainable winners. These are rare. They win for decades. Their growth is steady. Their peace is intact. Their identity is anchored. Their relationships survive the climb. They build empires without losing their humanity. They scale mountains without sacrificing what matters.

Sustainable winners can say with authenticity and conviction:

"I rise without losing myself."

"I grow without abandoning what matters."

"I succeed without collapsing internally."

"I build without breaking my life."

That kind of success is not accidental. It is designed. It results from intentional choices, strategic boundaries, and consistent practices that protect the core while expanding the reach.

Biblical Example: Joseph — A Life Built Before a Moment Arrived

Joseph didn't become powerful because he dreamed big. He became powerful because his inner life was built first. His character development preceded his career advancement, creating a foundation that could withstand both adversity and prosperity.

Before influence came, Joseph developed resilience in the pit. Before authority came, he practiced integrity in Potiphar's house. Before promotion came, he learned emotional control through betrayal, rejection, and injustice. Before command came, he cultivated wisdom, discipline, and restraint. Each challenge was forming the leader who would eventually save nations.

Joseph didn't rise because opportunity found him. Joseph rose because when opportunity arrived, his life could carry it. His internal capacity matched his external responsibility. This alignment prevented the collapse that often accompanies rapid advancement.

Greatness isn't retained by the most gifted. It's retained by the most structured. The systems, boundaries, and practices that govern your life will determine whether your gifts create lasting impact or temporary impressions.

The Four Pillars of a Life That Won't Break

A sustainable high-performance life stands on four stabilizers. Remove any one, and success becomes fragile. Together, they create a platform that can support significant achievement without personal deterioration.

Identity comes first. Who you are must not fluctuate with wins and losses. If identity is tied to performance, pressure will always feel threatening. When you know who you are apart from results, you can pursue excellence without existential anxiety. Your worth is established before your work begins.

Values come next. Values determine what you refuse to sacrifice to win. Without them, success consumes everything in its path. Values create non-negotiables that protect what matters most—integrity, family, health, faith—even when opportunities tempt compromise. They are the guardrails that keep ambition on a sustainable path.

Boundaries create protection. They guard your time, energy, relationships, and focus. Without boundaries, the world will gladly overrun your life. Boundaries aren't selfish—they're stewardship. They ensure that your most valuable resources are directed toward your highest priorities rather than scattered across endless demands.

Rhythms create consistency. Rhythms stabilize effort, energy, and recovery so performance becomes predictable—not emotional. They transform discipline from a daily struggle into a natural flow. These patterns of work, rest, connection, and renewal ensure that high output doesn't lead to eventual burnout.

With all four pillars in place, success becomes scalable and safe. You can pursue ambitious goals without compromising your core. You can expand your impact without imploding under pressure.

Why Burnout Is a Design Problem, Not a Work Problem

Burnout is rarely caused by working too hard. It's caused by working misaligned. People burn out when they're chasing goals that contradict their identity, values, or calling. The friction between who they are and what they're doing creates an unsustainable energy drain.

When the work fits the person, discipline gives energy. When the work contradicts the person, effort drains the soul. This explains why some people can work 60-hour weeks with enthusiasm while others burn out at 40 hours. Alignment matters more than hours.

A life that doesn't break is built intentionally—around who you are, not who the world demands you become. This authentic alignment creates resilience that withstands pressure, setbacks, and even success itself.

Eight Habits of Sustainable Winners

Sustainable winners show up consistently, not urgently. They don't spike effort emotionally—they maintain standards daily. Their excellence comes from reliable systems rather than motivational surges. They understand that consistency compounds while intensity often collapses.

They protect rest instead of dismissing it. Rest is not weakness; it is recovery and wisdom. They recognize that strategic disengagement increases capacity rather than reducing it. Their rhythms of work and renewal create sustainable output over decades.

They invest in relationships. They understand that isolation kills endurance. They build communities that provide support, accountability, perspective, and belonging. Their connections become resources that sustain them through challenges and celebrate their victories.

They refuse to hide behind achievement. Success is an expression of identity, not a substitute for it. They do the inner work required to know themselves apart from results. This self-awareness prevents the common cycle of using accomplishment to mask insecurity.

They train emotional discipline. Feelings are acknowledged but never allowed to lead. They develop the capacity to feel fear without fleeing, feel doubt without quitting, feel fatigue without stopping. This emotional regulation prevents the volatility that derails many high-achievers.

They communicate boundaries clearly and early. Protecting purpose always matters more than pleasing people. They establish expectations that honor their mission without apology. This clarity prevents the resentment that builds when boundaries are unclear or inconsistent.

They simplify decision-making through systems and routines. Fewer decisions reduce stress and preserve energy. They automate what doesn't require creativity and establish protocols that eliminate unnecessary friction. This efficiency creates mental space for high-value thinking.

They pursue growth beyond their career. They build a better person, not just a better résumé. Their development spans intellectual, spiritual, relational, and physical dimensions. This holistic approach creates a life where success enhances rather than diminishes wholeness.

Sustainable winners don't wait for life to get easier. They build lives that can handle difficulty. Their resilience comes not from avoiding challenges but from creating systems that absorb and transform them.

Systems Make Greatness Sustainable

Champions do not rely on motivation. They rely on systems. Motivation fluctuates daily while systems provide consistency regardless of emotional state. The infrastructure of excellence removes the need for constant willpower.

Systems stabilize effort, regulate energy, simplify decisions, and protect focus. When emotion is high or low, systems keep execution steady. They transform aspirational goals into actionable processes that produce predictable results. They make excellence habitual rather than heroic.

If you rely on feelings, you will always be inconsistent. If you rely on systems, you become inevitable. Your outcomes become a matter of process rather than chance. Your success becomes reproducible rather than occasional.

Systems don't restrict greatness. They protect it. Rather than limiting potential, they create the conditions where potential can be fully expressed without the typical consequences of burnout, relationship damage, or identity distortion.

Values: What You Refuse to Lose to Win

A life that doesn't break is anchored to clear values. Values answer this question: What matters more than success? This clarity creates boundaries around ambition that prevent it from becoming destructive.

Without values, ambition will sacrifice integrity, relationships, peace, faith, and identity on the altar of results. With values, success becomes additive instead of destructive. Your achievements enhance rather than erode what matters most.

If you do not choose your values intentionally, pressure will choose them for you. In moments of decision, whatever you truly value will determine your choices—regardless of what you claim to value. This is why clarifying and internalizing your core values before crisis moments is essential.

Boundaries Are the Price of Longevity

Without boundaries, expectations run your life. Distraction becomes normal. Resentment builds quietly. Overwhelm becomes permanent. The absence of limits creates a life where everything and everyone has access to your most valuable resources— attention, energy, and time.

Boundaries are not walls—they are guardrails. They don't isolate you from opportunity; they protect you from distraction. They don't limit your impact; they focus it. They create the conditions where your best work can emerge consistently.

They protect your mission, your energy, your peace, and your relationships. Anyone without boundaries eventually loses focus, direction, and joy. The temporary discomfort of setting limits prevents the permanent damage of living without them.

If what you are building is worth anything, it is worth protecting. Your mission deserves defense against the countless forces that would dilute or derail it. Boundaries are that defense system.

Rhythms Create Readiness

Greatness is not accidental. It is rhythmic. The most successful people in any field operate according to intentional patterns that maximize their strengths and minimize their vulnerabilities. These rhythms create predictability in an unpredictable world.

You don't rise to the level of passion. You rise to the level of patterns. What you do consistently will always outperform what you do occasionally, no matter how inspired. Your daily, weekly, and seasonal rhythms determine your results more than your aspirations.

A life that doesn't break includes rhythms for grounding, training, recovery, reflection, strategy, and celebration. These rhythms prevent emotional volatility and decision fatigue. They ensure that you're operating from a place of strength rather than depletion.

Strong rhythms produce predictable performance. Weak rhythms produce collapse. The difference between sustainable success and burnout often comes down to the quality of your operational rhythms.

Alignment Over Balance

Balance suggests equal attention everywhere. Alignment suggests intentional support of purpose. The pursuit of perfect balance often creates mediocrity across all domains, while alignment creates excellence that serves a unified mission.

The goal is not fifty-fifty between work and rest. The goal is one hundred percent purpose across every area of life. When each element of your life reinforces rather than competes with the others, you create a synergy that multiplies impact without dividing attention.

Alignment means relationships sharpen you. Work energizes you. Rest renews you. Habits reinforce identity. Challenges develop you. Boundaries protect you. Faith or values anchor you. Each component serves the whole rather than draining it.

When everything serves the mission instead of competing with it, you don't just win—you win without breaking. Your success becomes sustainable because it flows from a life designed for endurance, not just performance.

Reflection Questions

1. Which areas of my life are currently strong enough to support long-term success—and which would collapse under pressure? Where do I need to strengthen my foundation before adding more weight?

2. What are my non-negotiable values—what will I refuse to lose to win? How can I ensure these values guide my decisions under pressure?

3. Where do I need clearer boundaries to protect energy, peace, or purpose? What specific limits would prevent burnout without limiting impact?

4. What systems or routines would make discipline automatic instead of emotional? How can I reduce decision fatigue through better infrastructure?

5. Which relationships help me rise—and which quietly pull me away from who I am becoming? How can I invest more in connections that strengthen rather than strain my mission?

Closing Declaration

I refuse to build success that costs me my identity. I commit to building a life that can carry greatness. My achievements will enhance rather than erode what matters most.

My foundation is solid. My values are clear. My boundaries are strong. My rhythms sustain me. I am creating success that serves my purpose rather than consuming it.

I do not chase outcomes—I steward alignment. I will not burn out—I will endure. My impact will grow without requiring my collapse. My influence will expand without demanding my wholeness.

I am a Missionpreneur, and I am building a life that won't break me.

CHAPTER 17

SYSTEMS OVER SUPERSTARS

Why Structure Protects Legacy When Talent Is No Longer Enough

Superstars build moments.

Systems build movements.

Most legacies do not collapse because of bad intentions, poor vision, or lack of talent. They collapse because too much depended on too few. When an organization, family enterprise, ministry, or movement relies heavily on exceptional individuals rather than repeatable structure, fragility is guaranteed. This vulnerability remains invisible until crisis strikes, revealing the structural weaknesses that existed all along. The most dangerous aspect is that these dependencies often masquerade as strengths until they suddenly become liabilities.

Missionpreneurs understand a sobering truth early:

If excellence requires exceptional people, it is not sustainable.

Legacy is not protected by personality.

Legacy is protected by structure.

The Superstar Trap

Superstars are intoxicating. They deliver fast results, attract attention, and create the illusion of health. They step in, fix problems, close gaps, and carry weight others cannot—at least for a while. Their presence often becomes the unspoken strategy of the organization, creating a false sense of security that masks underlying structural deficiencies. The immediate results they produce can blind leadership to the long-term vulnerabilities being created.

But when organizations depend on one gifted leader, one irreplaceable employee, or one dominant personality, the system quietly weakens underneath them. The mission appears strong while the foundation erodes. Teams begin to develop unhealthy dependencies, waiting for direction rather than taking initiative. Decision-making bottlenecks form around key individuals, slowing organizational responsiveness and adaptability.

When that person leaves, falters, burns out, gets promoted, relocates, or simply has a bad season, everything stalls. The vacuum created by their absence reveals how much of the operational framework existed only in their mind. Recovery isn't simply about replacing talent—it requires rebuilding entire processes that were never properly documented or distributed.

Superstars scale results quickly.

They also scale risk.

Systems scale reliability.

The goal of Missionpreneur leadership is not to eliminate excellence—it is to remove dependence on singular excellence. True organizational strength comes from excellence that can be replicated, transferred, and maintained regardless of which individuals occupy specific roles. This distinction transforms excellence from a personality-dependent quality to a structural characteristic of the organization itself.

Why Leaders Default to Superstars

Most leaders do not rely on superstars out of ego. They do it out of pressure. Systems feel slow. Training feels inefficient. Documentation feels tedious. It feels easier to lean on the person who already knows how to do it, already performs at a high level, already understands the culture. The quarterly targets, immediate deadlines, and pressing demands create an environment where the path of least resistance is to deploy your best people rather than develop your best processes.

Speed today feels like progress. The immediate results create positive feedback loops that reinforce dependency on key performers. This short-term thinking becomes embedded in organizational culture, making it increasingly difficult to invest in longer-term systemic solutions that might initially slow productivity.

But speed without structure creates vulnerability tomorrow. When crises emerge or transitions occur, the absence of systems means rebuilding from scratch rather than relying on established frameworks. What seemed like efficiency becomes the very source of organizational paralysis.

Missionpreneurs are willing to delay speed to gain stability. They are not seduced by quick wins that endanger long-term endurance. They think beyond the next quarter, season, or campaign. They think generationally. This longer time horizon fundamentally changes how they evaluate success, prioritize resources, and build organizational capacity that transcends any single leader's tenure or contribution.

Charisma Is Not a Strategy

Charisma motivates people in moments of urgency. Systems govern behavior when urgency fades. While charismatic leadership can inspire immediate action and alignment, it cannot sustain consistent performance across different contexts and timeframes. The emotional energy that drives charismatic influence inevitably fluctuates, creating inconsistent results when used as a primary leadership mechanism.

Charisma is powerful in crisis. Systems preserve mission during transition. The very qualities that make charismatic leaders effective during high-pressure situations—decisiveness, emotional intensity, personal magnetism—often become liabilities during stable periods when methodical execution matters more than inspirational vision. The organization becomes conditioned to require emotional catalysts rather than disciplined processes.

When organizations rely on charisma without structure, decision-making becomes inconsistent. Expectations shift depending on who is present. Accountability erodes because standards are interpreted, not defined. Team members learn to navigate personalities rather than processes, creating inefficiencies and confusion that compound over time. This ambiguity creates hidden costs in productivity, morale, and organizational clarity.

Missionpreneurs refuse to build organizations that only function when "the right person" is in the room. They know that if leadership presence is required for alignment, alignment is not embedded. True organizational health is measured not by performance when key leaders are present, but by consistency when they are absent. This principle fundamentally reshapes how we evaluate leadership effectiveness and organizational maturity.

Systems Are Leadership in Written Form

A system is simply leadership made repeatable. It captures the wisdom, priorities, and values of leadership in a format that can be transferred, scaled, and implemented consistently across the organization. Well-designed systems don't replace leadership judgment—they amplify it by extending its reach beyond the physical presence of any individual leader.

Systems answer questions people ask silently every day: Who decides this? How is work done here? What does success look like? What happens when standards are violated? How does authority flow? These unspoken questions consume enormous mental and emotional energy when left unanswered. Clear systems liberate this energy for productive work rather than navigational confusion.

If leaders do not answer these questions proactively, chaos will answer them reactively—and chaos is never aligned with mission. The vacuum created by undefined systems will always be filled, but rarely with solutions that advance organizational purpose. Instead, informal workarounds, personal interpretations, and inconsistent practices emerge to fill the void, creating hidden conflicts with stated values.

Systems remove guesswork. They convert values into behaviors. They make clarity portable. When properly designed, they don't constrain creativity—they channel it toward mission-aligned outcomes. By establishing clear boundaries and expectations, systems actually create the safety needed for appropriate risk-taking and innovation within defined parameters.

This is why Missionpreneurs document—not to control, but to care. Documentation is not bureaucracy; it is compassion for the next leader. It represents a profound act of stewardship that acknowledges the temporary nature of our individual contributions and the enduring importance of the mission we serve. Through documentation, we transfer not just information but insight, context, and wisdom to those who will carry the work forward.

The Hidden Cost of Unspoken Knowledge

When knowledge lives only in people's heads, training slows, mistakes multiply, and frustration rises. What feels like efficiency to an expert becomes confusion to everyone else. The tacit knowledge that experienced team members take for granted becomes an invisible barrier to new contributors, creating unnecessary learning curves and performance gaps that could be avoided through proper documentation.

Unspoken knowledge creates dependency. It turns experienced leaders into bottlenecks and new leaders into bystanders. The mission stalls waiting for permission, interpretation, or rescue. This dependency cycle reinforces unhealthy power dynamics where information becomes currency and gatekeeping becomes normalized. Over time, this creates silos of expertise that fragment organizational effectiveness and resilience.

The true cost manifests in three critical dimensions: operational continuity suffers when key knowledge holders are unavailable; onboarding efficiency decreases as each new team member must rediscover institutional knowledge through trial and error; and innovation stagnates when foundational understanding remains trapped in isolated minds rather than becoming a platform for collective advancement.

Missionpreneurs document because they believe legacy matters beyond themselves. They refuse to hoard understanding. They externalize wisdom so others can build upon it. This commitment to knowledge transfer isn't just about operational efficiency—it reflects a fundamental belief about stewardship and the temporary nature of individual leadership within an enduring mission. By making implicit knowledge explicit, they create the conditions for exponential rather than linear growth.

The Four Systems Every Missionpreneur Must Build

Every enduring enterprise—family, ministry, business, or institution—requires four foundational systems. These interconnected frameworks create the infrastructure that supports sustainable mission advancement across generations of leadership. Their absence isn't immediately obvious during stable periods but becomes catastrophically evident during transitions or crises.

Decision systems clarify authority, boundaries, and escalation paths. They remove ambiguity about who decides what and when. Effective decision systems balance centralization and distribution appropriately, ensuring decisions are made at the right level with the right input. They establish clear thresholds for when decisions require additional approval, creating appropriate guardrails without unnecessary bottlenecks.

Training systems define how people learn, not just what they do. They create shared language and expectations. Rather than relying on osmosis or observation, intentional training systems accelerate competency development and cultural integration. These systems include not just initial training but ongoing development pathways that continuously elevate capabilities as the organization evolves. They transform individual expertise into institutional knowledge.

Accountability systems establish standards, feedback loops, and consequences. They protect fairness and trust. Well-designed accountability frameworks ensure that performance expectations are clear, measurement is consistent, and responses to both success and failure are proportionate and predictable. They create the psychological safety necessary for healthy risk-taking by establishing clear boundaries and consequences.

Succession systems prepare leadership transfer before it is required, not after crisis hits. They include identification of potential successors, intentional development of future leaders, and clear transition protocols. Effective succession systems treat leadership development as an ongoing organizational priority rather than a reactive response to impending departures. They ensure that leadership transitions strengthen rather than disrupt mission momentum.

If even one of these systems is missing, legacy is exposed. The interdependence of these frameworks means weakness in one area compromises the effectiveness of the others. Decision clarity without accountability creates risk. Training without succession planning creates short-term thinking. Accountability without clear decision authority creates confusion. Only when all four systems function in harmony can an organization truly transcend its founders and current leadership.

When Superstars Become Bottlenecks

Ironically, the most talented people often restrict growth unintentionally. Because others defer to them. Because they solve problems personally. Because they resist documentation in the name of speed. Their capability becomes the very thing that limits organizational capacity as processes, decisions, and knowledge flow through a single point of control. What begins as a solution gradually transforms into the primary constraint.

The cycle typically begins with positive intentions—high performers stepping in to ensure quality, maintain standards, or accelerate results. However, this intervention pattern gradually creates learned helplessness throughout the organization. Team members stop developing solutions because the superstar will eventually provide them. Initiative diminishes as dependency increases. The organization's problem-solving muscles atrophy while the superstar's grow stronger.

Over time, talent without structure produces exhaustion—not just in the superstar, but in everyone waiting on them. The bottlenecks create frustration on both sides: the high performer feels overburdened while team members feel disempowered. This mutual frustration often manifests as tension, misalignment, and eventually disengagement as the relationship between the superstar and the organization becomes increasingly dysfunctional.

Missionpreneurs teach high performers to multiply themselves through systems, not build empires around their ability. Great leaders are not threatened by replacement—they prepare for it. This mindset shift transforms how high-capacity individuals measure their success: not by personal productivity but by organizational capability, not by problems solved but by problem-solvers developed, not by personal indispensability but by system reliability that transcends their individual contribution.

Systems Create Fairness

Without systems, discipline feels personal, promotions feel political, and decisions feel arbitrary. People do not trust environments where rules shift based on personality, emotion, or favoritism. This inconsistency creates a culture of uncertainty where team members focus more on relationship management than mission advancement. The resulting environment rewards political savvy over performance and connection over contribution.

With systems, expectations are clear, accountability is consistent, and trust increases. People thrive in clarity—even when clarity is demanding. When team members understand how decisions are made, how performance is evaluated, and how advancement occurs, they can focus their energy on contribution rather than navigation. This transparency creates psychological safety that enables appropriate risk-taking and innovation.

Systems remove bias. They protect dignity. They reinforce justice. By establishing consistent frameworks that apply equally to all team members regardless of position, personality, or history, systems create the foundation for true meritocracy. They ensure that organizational rewards and consequences flow from performance rather than preference, creating an environment where contribution is recognized and excellence is rewarded regardless of who delivers it.

The fairness created by well-designed systems becomes a powerful competitive advantage in attracting and retaining talent. High-performing individuals are drawn to environments where their contribution will be recognized and rewarded based on merit rather than politics. This attraction of talent creates a virtuous cycle where system-driven fairness enables the organization to access higher levels of human capacity.

Systems Protect Culture

Culture is not what leaders say—it is what systems reinforce. The stated values and aspirations of an organization mean little if the operational systems reward contradictory behaviors. Systems are the invisible architecture that shapes daily decisions, priorities, and interactions. They determine which behaviors advance careers, which mistakes are tolerated, and which achievements are celebrated, regardless of the language used in mission statements.

If systems reward speed over integrity, results over character, or production over alignment, culture will drift no matter how strong the values statements are. The gap between stated values and operational reality creates cynicism that erodes trust and engagement. Team members quickly learn to respond to the incentives embedded in systems rather than the aspirations articulated in vision documents.

Effective cultural systems align rewards, recognition, advancement, and correction with stated values. They ensure that

217

what gets measured, celebrated, and compensated reflects the organization's core beliefs rather than contradicting them. This alignment creates authenticity that resonates with both internal stakeholders and external constituencies, building trust through consistency rather than rhetoric.

Missionpreneurs let systems guard culture when leadership presence is absent. They design culture to survive leadership change. This approach acknowledges that sustainable culture cannot depend on charismatic reinforcement or personal example alone—it must be embedded in the operational fabric of the organization. By systematizing cultural reinforcement, they ensure that values transcend any individual leader's tenure or influence.

Biblical Parallel: Jethro and Moses

Moses was a superstar. He carried vision, authority, and responsibility. People lined up daily for his judgment. The mission depended entirely on him—until Jethro intervened. This pattern of centralized leadership initially seemed effective but gradually created unsustainable strain on both the leader and the community. The bottleneck created by Moses' singular authority threatened the very mission he was committed to advancing.

Jethro recognized the danger immediately. "What you are doing is not good," he said. Moses was burning out, and the people were growing weary. The wisdom in Jethro's observation was recognizing that even divinely appointed leadership requires appropriate structure to function effectively. His concern addressed not just Moses' personal sustainability but the health of the entire community dependent on accessible leadership.

Jethro did not question Moses' calling. He questioned Moses' system. This critical distinction highlights that systems critique is not leadership rejection—it is leadership support. By focusing on the structural framework rather than the leader's legitimacy, Jethro created space for constructive change without undermining Moses' authority or vision. His approach demonstrates how systems thinking enhances rather than diminishes leadership effectiveness.

By distributing authority, creating structure, and establishing clear layers of leadership, the mission became sustainable. Moses remained faithful—but no longer central to every decision. The resulting framework maintained alignment with Moses' vision and values while dramatically expanding operational capacity. This biblical example provides a powerful template for how authority can be distributed without being diminished, and how systems enhance rather than replace inspired leadership.

God's work accelerated when systems replaced singular dependence. This spiritual principle reveals that proper structure doesn't constrain divine purpose—it enables it. The implementation of appropriate systems actually created greater capacity for spiritual impact by removing unnecessary bottlenecks and expanding the community's ability to address needs efficiently. This pattern of system-enabled mission advancement appears consistently throughout scripture and history.

From Heroes to Multipliers

Missionpreneurs fundamentally redefine what constitutes true greatness in organizational leadership. This redefinition challenges conventional wisdom about leadership value and organizational sustainability. The measure of exceptional leadership lies not in being constantly needed, but in creating structures that thrive beyond any individual.

Greatness is not being needed everywhere.

Greatness is being replaced everywhere.

Leaders who desperately cling to indispensability do not protect their legacy—they severely limit it. This attachment to being irreplaceable creates organizational vulnerability rather than strength. If every critical function, decision, or process depends on your presence, nothing truly belongs to the next generation of leadership or stakeholders.

Systems represent the strategic mechanism through which visionary leaders release operational control without sacrificing mission alignment. Well-designed systems encode values, standardize excellence, and ensure continuity through inevitable transitions. They transform individual brilliance into organizational intelligence.

Systemization Is Humility in Action

Building robust systems communicates something profoundly important about leadership posture and organizational values. It declares unequivocally, "This mission matters beyond my tenure." It boldly asserts, "Others will carry this vision forward with integrity." It humbly admits, "I am not the centerpiece of this organizational story."

Systemization stands as one of the most selfless acts of authentic leadership available to Missionpreneurs. It deliberately prioritizes organizational continuity over personal recognition, generational legacy over immediate ego gratification, and faithful obedience to mission over temporary admiration from peers. This approach fundamentally transforms how value is created and sustained.

The System Dependency Test: Evaluating Organizational Resilience

Every committed Missionpreneur must evaluate their organization honestly and thoroughly. This evaluation requires courageous self-assessment and organizational transparency. The dependency test reveals structural vulnerabilities that threaten long-term mission fulfillment.

What critical functions break down when a key person becomes unexpectedly unavailable? Where does essential operational knowledge live exclusively in one individual's experience? Which crucial processes remain undocumented or inconsistently followed? Which strategic decisions still require one personality's presence to move forward?

Every identified dependency point represents a significant legacy risk to the organization. These vulnerabilities create unnecessary fragility that jeopardizes mission continuity. Systems exist primarily to eliminate this organizational fragility—not merely to enhance performance metrics.

Why Systems Outlast Even Exceptional Talent

Individual talent inevitably ages. Personal energy naturally fluctuates through different life seasons. Family circumstances change unexpectedly. Professional seasons eventually end. These realities affect even the most dedicated leaders.

Well-designed systems, however, endure beyond individual limitations. They create organizational memory and operational consistency that transcends personnel changes. Systems allow average, properly trained people to achieve extraordinary consistency in delivering mission-critical outcomes.

Systems create organizational environments where excellence becomes normal, not heroic. Missionpreneurs reject building organizations that require perpetual extraordinary effort just to maintain basic functions. Instead, we build resilient systems that continue functioning effectively even during ordinary organizational changes and transitions.

Reflection Questions for Missionpreneurs

1. Where in my leadership approach am I primarily relying on exceptional people instead of robust structural systems?
2. Which critical roles or strategic decisions would immediately stall if one key person stepped away unexpectedly?
3. What specialized organizational knowledge must be documented immediately to protect operational continuity?
4. Do our current systems authentically reinforce our stated organizational values—or subtly undermine them?
5. What would fundamentally change in my leadership approach if I measured success primarily by how systematically replaceable I become?

Closing Declaration

I firmly refuse to build fragile organizational success around exceptional individuals alone. I wholeheartedly commit to building comprehensive systems that protect our mission beyond the limitations of personalities. This commitment shapes my daily leadership decisions.

Exceptional talent may effectively start organizational fires of innovation and impact.

But only well-designed systems keep those fires burning consistently across multiple generations.

My leadership effectiveness is not ultimately measured by how personally needed I am—

but by how seamlessly and faithfully the mission survives and thrives without my direct involvement.

I am a Missionpreneur, and I deliberately build sustainable systems—not dependent superstars.

CHAPTER 18

SUCCESSION WITHOUT FRACTURE

How to Transfer Leadership Without Destroying What You Built

Most legacies do not fail in creation. They fail in transition. The critical moment of vulnerability comes not during the building phase but when authority changes hands. This transition represents perhaps the most significant test of a mission's sustainability.

Buildings can be strong. Vision can be clear. Culture can be vibrant. Momentum can be real. Yet everything can fracture in a single season—not because the mission was wrong, but because the handoff was mishandled. What took decades to construct can unravel in months when succession planning fails.

Succession is rarely derailed by lack of talent. It is derailed by lack of preparation, clarity, and courage. The technical aspects of leadership transition are seldom the breaking point—it's the emotional and relational dimensions that cause fractures when not properly addressed.

Missionpreneurs do not wait for crisis, conflict, illness, or exhaustion to talk about succession. They build it long before it is needed—while leadership is strong, relationships are healthy, and vision is clear. They view succession planning as an integral component of organizational strategy rather than a reaction to inevitable change.

Succession done well does not end leadership. It completes it. Far from diminishing a leader's impact, thoughtful transition multiplies it across generations and extends influence far beyond what one person could achieve in a single lifetime of leadership.

Why Succession Feels So Threatening

Succession confronts a leader's deepest internal fears. These anxieties often remain unacknowledged but powerfully influence decision-making around leadership transition. The emotional dimensions of succession frequently overshadow the strategic ones.

Fear of losing relevance. Fear of losing control. Fear of losing identity. Fear of becoming unnecessary. Fear of being forgotten. These concerns strike at the core of a leader's self-perception and can paralyze even the most forward-thinking Missionpreneur when succession planning begins.

Leadership becomes personal when legacy feels uncertain. What began as stewardship subtly shifts into possession. The mission that was once held with open hands gradually becomes clutched with closed fists, not from malice but from deep-seated insecurity about what comes next.

But here is the truth Missionpreneurs must face: Succession is not a referendum on your worth. It is confirmation of your faithfulness. The ability to release authority demonstrates that your leadership was never about you—it was always about the mission and its continuation.

If leadership cannot be transferred, it was never truly owned. It was merely held. True ownership manifests in the capacity to release authority with confidence, knowing the mission transcends any individual's tenure.

A leader who cannot release authority is not protecting legacy—they are revealing insecurity. This reluctance signals that personal identity has become too entangled with positional authority, compromising objective decision-making about organizational needs.

The High Cost of Avoidance

Most leadership fractures do not happen because someone made the wrong decision. They happen because leaders avoided the necessary conversation. Postponement, not poor planning, is the primary culprit in succession failures across mission-driven organizations.

Succession is postponed because "things are working." The timing feels awkward. The conversation feels uncomfortable. There is no immediate pressure. These seemingly reasonable justifications mask deeper anxieties and create the illusion that delay carries no consequences.

Avoidance buys temporary peace—but guarantees long-term chaos. The organizational cost of succession procrastination compounds over time, creating increasingly complex problems that become more difficult to resolve with each passing year.

When succession is ignored, power vacuums emerge. Informal influence replaces formal authority. Families divide. Teams form factions. Organizations fracture. Culture erodes. The absence of clear succession planning creates environments where political maneuvering replaces principled leadership.

Silence does not preserve unity. Silence guarantees confusion. What remains unsaid becomes the source of speculation, assumption, and misalignment. The vacuum created by leadership avoidance inevitably fills with competing narratives about the future.

Missionpreneurs understand that hard conversations held early prevent destructive conversations later. They recognize that the temporary discomfort of succession planning is infinitely preferable to the permanent damage of succession crises.

Succession Is a Process, Not an Event

Healthy succession never happens suddenly. It is gradual, intentional, visible, and unmistakable. It unfolds as a carefully orchestrated series of transitions rather than a single moment of authority transfer. This process-oriented approach allows for adjustment, learning, and relationship-building throughout the transition.

Missionpreneurs reject last-minute transitions. They understand that surprise transitions are almost always traumatic transitions. Abrupt leadership changes create organizational whiplash, erode trust, and destabilize even the healthiest cultures.

Succession unfolds through:

- ◆ Shared authority over time, with increasing responsibility gradually transferred to successors
- ◆ Increasing responsibility with accountability, allowing emerging leaders to make consequential decisions while still receiving guidance
- ◆ Public affirmation of emerging leaders, signaling to the entire organization who carries authority and who has the founder's confidence
- ◆ Clear communication about direction and roles, eliminating ambiguity about decision rights and reporting relationships

When succession is healthy, no one is shocked. The transition feels natural because it has been visible, discussed, and demonstrated over an extended period. The formal handover of authority merely confirms what everyone already understands.

When succession is unhealthy, everyone is confused. Uncertainty prevails about who holds decision rights, whose vision guides strategy, and how authority flows through the organization. This confusion creates paralysis and undermines confidence in the future.

The Five-Phase Succession Timeline

Succession without fracture follows a recognizable path. Understanding these phases allows Missionpreneurs to track progress, identify gaps, and ensure that no critical step is overlooked in the transition process.

Phase 1: Identification

Potential successors are discerned—not assumed. This is not about favoritism, bloodline, or convenience. It is about calling, character, capacity, and chemistry with the mission. This phase requires honest assessment of leadership potential, separate from personal affection or family obligation.

Phase 2: Preparation

Training, testing, correction, and stretching occur. Potential successors are exposed to pressure, decision-making, conflict, and responsibility long before authority is transferred. This developmental phase builds capacity through progressive challenges and honest feedback about performance.

Phase 3: Shared Authority

Decision-making is intentionally distributed. The founder resists the urge to override. Trust becomes visible. Mistakes become part of training—not reasons for control. This phase tests both the successor's readiness and the founder's willingness to truly release authority rather than merely delegate tasks.

Phase 4: Transfer

Authority changes hands clearly, publicly, and unmistakably. Titles, decision rights, and accountability structures are updated. There is no confusion about who leads. This formal transfer creates organizational clarity and prevents the formation of competing power centers or shadow authority structures.

Phase 5: Support

Outgoing leaders advise without undermining. They offer wisdom without interference. They protect unity by staying in their lane. This phase requires extraordinary discipline from founders, who must resist the temptation to reclaim authority when disagreements arise about direction or decisions.

The longer Phase 1 is delayed, the more painful Phase 4 becomes. Early identification of potential successors allows for gradual, natural transition. Postponement compresses the process, forcing rushed decisions and creating unnecessary organizational trauma.

The Danger of Dying in the Chair

Some leaders never release authority—not because they cannot, but because they will not. This choice, often rationalized as dedication or irreplaceability, reveals a fundamental misunderstanding of leadership's ultimate purpose: to create sustainable impact beyond the founder's tenure.

They remain centralized. They remain indispensable. They remain emotionally tethered to control. Their identity becomes so fused with their role that separation feels impossible, creating organizational dependency that becomes increasingly unhealthy over time.

The organization functions while they are present—but collapses when they are gone. Systems, decisions, and relationships all depend on the founder's direct involvement, creating an institutional brittleness that cannot withstand their absence. The very strength of their leadership becomes the organization's greatest vulnerability.

This is not heroic leadership. It is leadership that forgot its assignment. True leadership builds systems, develops people, and creates cultures that thrive beyond the founder's active involvement. Anything less reflects a mission subordinated to ego.

Missionpreneurs understand that leadership held too long becomes self-serving rather than sacrificial. Staying past your season is not faithfulness—it is fear dressed up as loyalty. The courage to release authority at the right time demonstrates that the mission has always been more important than personal position or power.

Biblical Example: Moses and Joshua

Moses did not lose identity by preparing Joshua. He fulfilled it. This biblical succession model demonstrates how intentional leadership transition preserves mission integrity while honoring both the departing and emerging leader. The handoff between Moses and Joshua provides timeless principles for Missionpreneurs seeking seamless succession.

God instructed Moses to publicly commission Joshua. Authority was transferred clearly. The people saw it. The leaders recognized it. The mission continued without confusion. This visible, unmistakable transfer eliminated any question about who carried authority after Moses stepped aside.

Moses did not weaken legacy by releasing leadership. He preserved it. His willingness to identify, prepare, and commission a successor ensured that his life's work would continue beyond his lifetime. Moses understood that holding on too long would jeopardize everything he had built.

Joshua did not replace Moses. He continued what Moses began. This continuity-with-distinction model shows how healthy succession honors the foundation laid by founders while allowing new leaders to address new challenges with fresh approaches. The mission remained constant while leadership styles appropriately evolved.

That is succession without fracture. The transition from Moses to Joshua demonstrates how leadership can change hands without diminishing impact, dividing followers, or diluting mission focus. It establishes a pattern that Missionpreneurs can follow with confidence.

When Family Complicates Succession

Succession becomes most complex when family is involved. The intertwining of business relationships with family dynamics creates layers of complexity that require exceptional clarity, courage, and communication to navigate successfully. Family business succession demands even greater intentionality than other leadership transitions.

Love clouds judgment. Avoidance amplifies resentment. Silence creates entitlement. These emotional dynamics can undermine even the most carefully designed succession plans when family relationships complicate organizational decisions about leadership and authority.

Missionpreneurs do not pretend this tension does not exist. They confront it with clarity. They recognize that failing to address family succession dynamics directly will inevitably create conflict, confusion, and potential mission failure down the road.

They separate:

- Relationship from role, ensuring that family connection alone never determines leadership position
- Love from leadership authority, making clear that affection and positional power operate in different dimensions
- Inheritance from governance, distinguishing between asset ownership and organizational decision-making rights

Family members may be loved equally—but they are not all called equally to lead. Clarity is not cruelty. It is protection. Honest assessment of leadership capacity within family systems prevents both relational damage and organizational dysfunction when expectations are misaligned.

Undefined expectations inside family systems destroy both relationships and missions. Assumptions about who will lead, how decisions will be made, and how authority will transition create invisible fault lines that eventually fracture under pressure. Explicit communication, though initially uncomfortable, prevents devastating misunderstandings later.

The Succession Covenant

Succession must be governed—not emotionally negotiated. Without clear parameters, succession decisions become vulnerable to relational pressure, emotional manipulation, and shifting circumstances. A formal framework provides stability during what can otherwise become a chaotic process.

Missionpreneurs establish succession covenants that define:

◆ Clear criteria for leadership readiness, establishing objective standards that potential successors must meet

◆ Defined timelines for transition, creating shared expectations about when authority will transfer

◆ Objective evaluation standards, removing personal bias from assessments of leadership capacity

◆ Accountability structures during and after transfer, ensuring that both outgoing and incoming leaders fulfill their responsibilities

Succession covenants remove personality from decision-making and replace it with purpose. They elevate mission above individual preference and create a framework for transition that transcends emotional reactions or relational dynamics. This governance approach maintains organizational integrity during leadership change.

They protect successors from resentment. They protect founders from regret. They protect the mission from fragmentation. By establishing clear boundaries, expectations, and processes, succession covenants create a path for healthy transition that honors all parties while preserving organizational health.

Succession Does Not Diminish the Founder

Founders often fear being forgotten once authority is released. This anxiety about legacy and relevance can become a significant barrier to timely succession planning. The fear of diminishment leads many founders to hold on too long, ironically undermining the very legacy they hope to preserve.

The opposite is true. Historical patterns demonstrate that founders who successfully transfer authority actually enhance their long-term impact and reputation. Their influence expands through those they've empowered rather than contracting through their absence.

Founders who hoard authority are remembered briefly—and blamed later. Founders who multiply leaders are remembered longer—and honored deeper. The paradox of succession is that releasing control actually strengthens legacy rather than weakening it.

Legacy is amplified by release, not preserved by retention. Each successor who builds upon the founder's foundation extends and magnifies the original vision. The founder who develops multiple leaders creates exponential impact that a single lifetime of leadership could never achieve.

History remembers those who finished well—not those who refused to finish. The final chapter of a founder's leadership story often determines how their entire contribution will be evaluated. A graceful exit that empowers others becomes the capstone of a well-lived leadership journey.

Succession Is How Culture Is Protected

Culture is most vulnerable during transition. The values, practices, and priorities that define an organization face their greatest test when leadership changes hands. Without intentional protection, cultural distinctives can quickly erode during succession, regardless of how strong they were previously.

When leadership change is unclear, standards slip. Vision fragments. Authority becomes informal. Trust erodes. Ambiguity creates an environment where cultural guardianship becomes diffuse, allowing mission drift to occur gradually but inexorably as leadership vacuums form.

But when succession is planned, culture survives leadership change intact. Direction remains clear. Accountability remains consistent. Unity remains strong. Intentional succession planning includes specific strategies for cultural preservation, ensuring that core values transcend individual leaders.

Missionpreneurs protect culture by planning transitions before pressure forces them. They recognize that emergency successions rarely preserve organizational distinctives effectively. By preparing successors who deeply understand and embody the mission's cultural DNA, they ensure continuity of both operation and identity.

The Fracture Point

Most organizational fractures occur at the same point. Understanding this pattern allows Missionpreneurs to recognize warning signs before irreparable damage occurs. The sequence of organizational breakdown follows a predictable trajectory when succession is mishandled.

Authority begins to shift informally. Power is implied but not assigned. Decision rights are unclear. Accountability disappears. This gradual dissolution of organizational clarity creates an environment where competing power centers emerge, trust erodes, and mission alignment fractures.

Missionpreneurs refuse informal leadership transitions. They make authority visible, verbal, and verifiable. They understand that ambiguity around leadership creates unnecessary conflict, confusion, and mission drift that undermines organizational health and effectiveness.

Ambiguity is the enemy of peace. When team members, stakeholders, and constituents cannot clearly identify who holds decision-making authority, anxiety permeates the organization. This uncertainty creates political maneuvering, faction formation, and the erosion of collaborative culture.

Succession Readiness Assessment

Every Missionpreneur must evaluate honestly and thoroughly whether their organization is prepared for leadership transition. This assessment isn't merely administrative—it's fundamental to ensuring mission continuity and organizational health beyond the founder's tenure. The answers reveal both strengths to leverage and vulnerabilities requiring immediate attention.

Is succession discussed openly as a natural part of organizational development, or is it avoided as an uncomfortable topic? Are potential successors being actively identified, mentored, and trained through intentional development programs, or are they merely assumed to be ready when needed? Is decision-making authority being shared deliberately through graduated responsibility, creating opportunities for growth? Would the organization continue to function effectively, maintain donor relationships, and pursue its mission without your daily involvement?

Any "no" answer is not a condemnation of leadership quality—but it is a significant warning sign that requires strategic attention. These indicators highlight areas where the mission's future sustainability may be at risk despite current operational success.

Ignoring these warning signs does not protect your legacy; it fundamentally endangers it. Responding to them proactively with courage and humility does more than preserve your work—it multiplies it across generations of impact.

Leading Through the Handoff

The final test of leadership is not how much you built or how large your organization grew under your guidance. It is not measured by financial metrics or program expansion alone, though these may reflect faithful stewardship.

It is how well you release what you built to those who will carry it forward. This transition represents the ultimate demonstration of whether you truly believe the mission transcends your personal involvement. The handoff reveals whether you've been building an organization or merely extending your personal platform.

Leaders who hand off well trust God with outcomes beyond their control. They celebrate emerging leadership publicly and consistently, creating legitimacy before transition occurs. They protect organizational unity even when ego is tempted to reassert control or question decisions. They resist the powerful urge to micromanage from the sidelines after authority has been transferred, understanding that their new role requires different boundaries.

Missionpreneurs understand that humility is most visible and most tested at the finish line. This final chapter often reveals the true character that has been present throughout the leadership journey but becomes unmistakably evident during transition.

Succession Is Spiritual Work

Succession is not merely operational or administrative. It is deeply spiritual work that tests core values and beliefs about purpose and identity. This process often triggers profound questions about personal worth, legacy definition, and future contribution that extend far beyond organizational charts.

It requires multilayered trust—trust in God's sovereignty over the organization's future, trust in people's development and capacity to lead differently but effectively, and trust that obedience to releasing control matters more than maintaining it. This trust must be practical and demonstrated through concrete actions, not merely affirmed in principle.

Letting go reveals whether leadership was ever truly about faithful stewardship of a temporary assignment or about self-fulfillment and personal validation. The difference becomes unmistakable during transition, regardless of the narrative maintained during active leadership.

Reflection Questions

1. Where am I avoiding necessary succession conversations because they feel uncomfortable or threatening to my current identity and role?
2. What specific fears surface when I think about being replaced, and how are these fears influencing my leadership decisions today?
3. Who is currently being prepared to lead in my place—and how intentionally structured is their development path? What specific responsibilities have I transferred to test their readiness?
4. Is authority being transferred clearly through documented processes or merely informally through casual conversations? Are stakeholders aware of the succession roadmap?
5. Would the mission survive intact if I stepped away tomorrow? What specific vulnerabilities exist that depend entirely on my presence or relationships?

Closing Declaration

Succession is not about replacement as though leadership were merely a position to fill. It is about continuation of purpose that transcends any individual contributor. The mission must outlive the missionpreneur for true impact to be realized.

I refuse to cling to authority at the expense of the mission's future. I recognize that holding on too long often damages what was built through years of sacrifice. I commit to prepare others systematically, release leadership incrementally, and finish well by celebrating others' success.

My worth is not measured by how long I maintain control or how indispensable I become—but by how well the mission continues without my direct involvement. True success is measured by organizational health after transition, not during my tenure alone.

If leadership ends with me because I failed to develop others, the mission ends with me regardless of my intentions or desires. That will not be my story or my legacy. I choose multiplication over addition.

I am a Missionpreneur, and I transfer leadership without fracture, ensuring continuity of purpose beyond my season of influence.

CHAPTER 19

TEACHING VISION WITHOUT
PASSING WEAKNESS

How to Multiply Strength Without Reproducing Blind Spots

Every leader passes down two things—whether they intend to or not: What they consciously teach and what they never confront. This duality shapes organizational culture more powerfully than mission statements or strategic plans. The unaddressed aspects of leadership often become the most defining legacy elements, creating patterns that outlive the leader's tenure.

Vision multiplies when strengths are transferred with clarity. Legacy collapses when weaknesses are left unnamed. The transmission of vision requires intentional communication of both what to pursue and what to avoid. Without this balanced approach, organizations risk perpetuating dysfunctional patterns under the guise of "honoring tradition."

Missionpreneurs understand a difficult but liberating truth: If you do not confront your blind spots, you will baptize them in the next generation. These normalized weaknesses become embedded in organizational DNA, often disguised as "the way we do things here." The cost of this avoidance compounds over time, creating systemic issues that become increasingly difficult to address.

What goes unexamined does not disappear. It reproduces. This reproduction happens through hiring practices, reward systems, decision-making frameworks, and the subtle social cues that communicate what truly matters in the organization. Unaddressed issues don't simply persist—they amplify across generations of leadership.

The Myth of "They'll Do It Better"

Many leaders comfort themselves with a quiet assumption: "The next generation will fix what I couldn't." This passive approach to organizational improvement relies on hope rather than intentional design. It places an unfair burden on successors who inherit systems they didn't create and problems they may not fully understand.

But improvement requires awareness. Without explicit identification of current limitations, successors lack the context needed to implement meaningful change. They may sense problems but struggle to diagnose root causes or distinguish between essential traditions and outdated practices.

Unexamined patterns replicate. Unchallenged habits repeat. Unspoken dysfunction hardens into culture. These organizational realities operate independently of good intentions, creating momentum that resists change. What begins as a temporary adaptation often becomes a permanent fixture without intentional intervention.

The next generation does not inherit your intentions. They inherit your systems, behaviors, defaults, and emotional reflexes. These operational realities carry more weight than mission statements or values posters. The lived experience of the organization—how decisions are actually made, how conflict is handled, how success is defined—forms the true inheritance.

Intentions die. Patterns live. The most well-meaning vision statements cannot overcome entrenched operational patterns. When leaders fail to align systems with stated values, the disconnect creates cynicism and erodes trust throughout the organization.

Missionpreneurs do not assume progress. They design it. This requires creating intentional systems for evaluation, feedback, and adaptation. Progress becomes a structured process rather than a hoped-for outcome, with clear mechanisms for identifying and addressing organizational blind spots.

Every Strength Has a Shadow

Leadership strengths always cast shadows. This paradox means that the very qualities that drive success also create vulnerability. Understanding this duality allows leaders to harness strengths while mitigating their potential negative impacts.

Vision can become impatience. Confidence can become arrogance. Urgency can become pressure. Loyalty can become favoritism. Discipline can become rigidity. Decisiveness can become dismissal. These transformations happen gradually, often imperceptibly, as strengths are applied without balanced accountability or contextual awareness.

The more effective the leader, the more dangerous the shadow—because success often silences feedback. High-performing leaders face a particular challenge: their effectiveness creates a feedback vacuum where team members become reluctant to raise concerns. This isolation increases the risk that strengths will drift into their shadow expressions without correction.

Missionpreneurs refuse the fantasy of "pure strengths." They examine the shadow so it cannot lead in silence. This requires creating structured opportunities for honest feedback and demonstrating receptivity to correction. By acknowledging the shadow aspects of their leadership, they create permission for others to speak truth without fear.

Ignoring the shadow does not make it holy. It makes it hidden. Hidden influences often exert more power than acknowledged ones. When leaders pretend their strengths have no downsides, they lose credibility and create organizational blind spots that undermine effectiveness.

Why Leaders Avoid Examining Weakness

Leaders often avoid naming weakness because of deeply rooted psychological and organizational factors. These avoidance patterns create significant barriers to growth and limit the leader's ability to build sustainable organizations.

♦ Exposure feels risky - acknowledging limitations seems to create vulnerability in competitive environments

♦ Authority feels fragile - many leaders believe their influence depends on perceived infallibility

♦ Vulnerability feels like loss - admitting weakness triggers fear of diminished respect or effectiveness

♦ Confidence is confused with infallibility - organizational cultures often reward certainty over humility

But here is the paradox: Unacknowledged weakness damages authority far more than acknowledged correction. When leaders pretend infallibility, they create impossible standards that eventually collapse under their own weight. The resulting credibility loss far exceeds what would have occurred through honest acknowledgment of limitations.

People trust leaders who are honest about growth. People withdraw from leaders who pretend perfection. This truth reflects basic human psychology—we connect with authenticity and distance ourselves from perceived deception. When leaders model growth-oriented vulnerability, they create psychological safety that enhances organizational performance.

Humility does not weaken leadership. Denial corrodes it. True authority comes not from projecting flawlessness but from demonstrating integrity. Leaders who acknowledge limitations while maintaining clear vision create environments where innovation and accountability can flourish simultaneously.

Blind Spots Are Not Moral Failures

Blind spots are not sins. They are limitations. This distinction helps leaders address weaknesses without unnecessary shame or defensiveness. Understanding blind spots as natural limitations rather than character flaws creates space for constructive improvement.

They develop when:

- Leaders move fast - rapid decision-making creates cognitive shortcuts that bypass thorough analysis
- Success accelerates - positive results reinforce existing approaches and discourage critical examination
- Responsibility expands - increasing demands stretch attention and create selective focus
- Feedback decreases - positional authority creates communication barriers that filter important information

Blind spots are a natural byproduct of influence. What matters is not having them—but handling them. Every leader has limitations; the differentiating factor is how systematically they work to identify and address these gaps. This approach transforms blind spots from leadership liabilities into growth opportunities.

Missionpreneurs build feedback into legacy so growth never stops when success starts. They create formal systems that ensure blind spots receive attention regardless of organizational performance. These mechanisms might include 360-degree reviews, external advisors, designated "truth-tellers," or structured evaluation processes that highlight potential blind spots.

Modeling vs. Imposing

There is a critical difference between teaching vision and enforcing methods. This distinction determines whether successors become innovative leaders or mere implementers.

Understanding this difference allows leaders to transfer vision without constraining future adaptation.

Modeling says:

"Here's how I led. Learn from what worked—and what didn't." This approach provides context and principles while acknowledging limitations. It invites critical thinking rather than mere replication and prepares successors for evolving challenges.

Imposing says:

"Do it exactly my way because it worked for me." This approach treats past success as a comprehensive blueprint rather than a contextual example. It creates rigid expectations that limit adaptation and innovation, ultimately undermining organizational resilience.

Modeling creates discernment. Imposing creates dependency. When leaders model rather than impose, they develop successors who can evaluate situations independently and apply principles appropriately. This discernment capability becomes increasingly valuable as organizational contexts evolve.

Modeling produces builders. Imposing produces imitators. Builders can construct new approaches based on foundational principles, while imitators can only replicate existing patterns. In rapidly changing environments, organizations need builders who can adapt while maintaining core identity.

Legacy requires builders. Sustainable organizations depend on leaders who can innovate while preserving essential values. By modeling rather than imposing, leaders develop successors who can navigate unforeseen challenges while maintaining organizational integrity.

The Courage to Name the Shadow

Missionpreneurs practice rare leadership courage. They engage in honest self-assessment that many leaders avoid, creating a culture of transparency that strengthens organizational health. This courage manifests in both private reflection and appropriate public acknowledgment.

They say out loud:

♦ "This decision cost more than I expected" - acknowledging miscalculations without defensiveness

♦ "I handled this poorly" - taking responsibility for leadership mistakes without excuses

♦ "My strength became pressure here" - recognizing when positive qualities created negative outcomes

♦ "Success blinded me in this season" - identifying how achievements created overconfidence or complacency

Naming the shadow removes its power. When weaknesses remain unacknowledged, they operate as hidden influences that shape decisions and culture without scrutiny. Naming creates awareness that enables intentional management rather than unconscious perpetuation.

When weakness is hidden, it leads quietly. When weakness is named, it loses authority. Hidden weaknesses exert disproportionate influence because they operate below the threshold of organizational awareness. Named weaknesses become manageable challenges rather than controlling forces.

Transparency is legacy protection. By naming shadows openly, leaders prevent these limitations from becoming embedded in organizational DNA. This transparency creates permission for

250

future leaders to address emerging blind spots without fear of violating organizational taboos.

Teaching Discernment, Not Dependence

The goal of leadership transfer is not compliance. It is discernment. Effective succession develops leaders who can think independently rather than merely implement established patterns. This capability becomes increasingly valuable as organizations navigate complex and changing environments.

Missionpreneurs teach the next generation:

- ◆ How to think biblically - applying timeless principles to contemporary challenges
- ◆ How to evaluate tradeoffs - making wise decisions when competing values create tension
- ◆ How to weigh timing - discerning when to act decisively and when to wait patiently
- ◆ How to make decisions without permission - taking appropriate initiative within clear boundaries

They do not want successors who ask, "What would you do?" forever. This dependency creates organizational bottlenecks and prevents adaptation. It also places unhealthy pressure on founding leaders to maintain involvement beyond appropriate transition points.

They want leaders who ask, "What is God requiring now?" This question shifts focus from past precedent to present discernment. It acknowledges that changing contexts require fresh application of enduring principles rather than rigid adherence to established methods.

Dependence freezes leadership. Discernment multiplies it. Organizations that cultivate discernment can adapt to changing circumstances while maintaining core identity. This adaptability creates resilience that sustains mission impact across generations of leadership.

Correction Is an Inheritance

Correction is one of the most loving legacies a leader can leave. Though often uncomfortable in the moment, constructive correction represents a significant investment in future leadership capacity. It demonstrates commitment to long-term organizational health rather than short-term relational comfort.

Correction says:

- ♦ "I trust you with truth" - demonstrating confidence in the recipient's maturity and potential
- ♦ "I value your future more than my image" - prioritizing development over personal comfort
- ♦ "I care enough to confront before damage accumulates" - preventing small issues from becoming major limitations

Avoiding correction feels kind—but it poisons the future quietly. When leaders prioritize temporary comfort over necessary truth, they allow harmful patterns to strengthen. This avoidance may preserve short-term harmony but creates long-term dysfunction that undermines organizational health.

Missionpreneurs correct early, clearly, and consistently—before patterns calcify into culture. They recognize that the longer an issue persists, the more difficult it becomes to address. By addressing concerns promptly, they prevent problematic behaviors from becoming normalized within the organizational environment.

The Weakness Transfer Audit (Blueprint Section)

Every Missionpreneur must slow down and ask: What patterns might I be unconsciously transferring to the next generation? This intentional examination requires temporarily suspending defensive responses to create space for honest assessment. It may benefit from external perspective through trusted advisors or formal assessment tools.

- ◆ What leadership habit has repeatedly caused tension? Look for recurring conflicts or consistent feedback that points to specific behavioral patterns.

- ◆ What feedback do I consistently resist? Pay attention to suggestions you automatically dismiss or explain away.

- ◆ Where do people become quiet around me? Notice topics or situations where team engagement suddenly decreases.

- ◆ What conflict keeps resurfacing under new names? Identify recurring issues that appear in different contexts but share common roots.

- ◆ Where does urgency override wisdom? Recognize patterns where speed consistently trumps thorough consideration.

Patterns expose shadows. What keeps repeating is asking to be examined. Repetition provides valuable diagnostic information about underlying issues. By tracking patterns over time, leaders can identify blind spots that might otherwise remain invisible despite their significant impact.

Separating Calling From Method

Calling is timeless. Methods are seasonal. This distinction allows organizations to maintain identity while adapting to changing contexts. Understanding the difference between fundamental purpose and specific implementation creates space for innovation without compromising core mission.

Missionpreneurs teach the why deeply—and hold the how loosely. They invest significant energy in transferring purpose, values, and vision while remaining flexible about specific strategies and tactics. This approach creates clarity about what must be preserved and what can evolve.

They explain the mission so clearly that successors can innovate without abandoning identity. This clarity creates freedom within boundaries—successors understand the non-negotiable elements of organizational identity while receiving permission to adapt methods to changing circumstances. This balance prevents both rigid preservation of outdated approaches and unnecessary abandonment of core purpose.

If successors must copy your methods exactly, the vision has been over-personalized. Excessive attachment to specific methodologies often indicates that the leader has conflated personal preference with organizational necessity. This confusion limits adaptation and creates unnecessary succession challenges.

Legacy multiplies when identity is preserved and methods evolve. Sustainable organizations maintain consistent purpose while continuously adapting implementation. This combination of stability and flexibility creates resilience that allows the mission to thrive across changing contexts.

Passing Wisdom Without Passing Wounds

Unhealed wounds bleed into leadership. Personal trauma and unresolved issues inevitably shape leadership behavior, often in ways that remain invisible to the leader while becoming obvious to others. These influences create distortions that undermine effectiveness and damage organizational culture.

Pain becomes policy. Fear becomes control. Ego becomes governance. Insecurity becomes urgency. These transformations occur subtly as leaders unconsciously structure organizations to protect themselves from reexperiencing past wounds. Without awareness, these protective mechanisms create dysfunctional systems that outlive their original purpose.

Missionpreneurs do the internal work so:

- ♦ Pain does not shape standards - ensuring that past hurts don't create unreasonable expectations
- ♦ Fear does not define boundaries - establishing appropriate limits based on wisdom rather than anxiety
- ♦ Ego does not drive decisions - separating personal validation needs from organizational requirements

Healing is not self-indulgence. Healing is legacy protection. Personal growth work directly impacts organizational health by preventing the transfer of dysfunction. This investment benefits not only the leader but everyone influenced by their leadership decisions and organizational culture.

You cannot protect the next generation from wounds you refuse to heal yourself. Unaddressed personal issues inevitably shape leadership behavior and organizational culture. By pursuing appropriate healing, leaders prevent their wounds from becoming organizational limitations that restrict future impact.

From Replication to Elevation: The True Purpose of Leadership Transfer

The goal of leadership transfer is not mere replication of what already exists. It is elevation—a deliberate process of raising capabilities, vision, and impact to new heights. When executed properly, succession becomes transformation rather than duplication, allowing organizations to evolve beyond their founder's original blueprint.

The next generation of leaders should be empowered and equipped to:

♦ See clearer—developing enhanced strategic vision that accounts for emerging opportunities and challenges
♦ Build stronger—creating more resilient systems and relationships that withstand market pressures
♦ Lead wiser—making decisions informed by both inherited wisdom and fresh perspective
♦ Finish healthier—achieving sustainable success without the burnout that often accompanies pioneering leadership

Legacy fundamentally fails when founders position themselves as the permanent benchmark against which all future leadership is measured. This approach creates an artificial ceiling that stifles innovation and limits organizational growth potential. True visionary leaders celebrate being surpassed by those they've mentored, understanding that this is the ultimate validation of their leadership investment.

Biblical Pattern: David and Solomon as Leadership Transfer Model

David was a visionary leader who established a kingdom through conquest and determination. Solomon inherited not just territory and authority, but a foundation upon which to build something even greater. This historical succession offers profound insights for modern leadership transition.

David meticulously prepared the vision for the temple and kingdom's future, but he also clearly named his limitations. He acknowledged where his leadership path was marked by necessary but costly conflict and bloodshed. Solomon was instructed not just in how to wield power effectively, but in how to exercise appropriate restraint—learning from both his father's strengths and weaknesses.

Through this process, vision was transferred with clarity and purpose. Crucially, weakness was acknowledged rather than normalized or institutionalized. That critical distinction preserved the kingdom's strength and set the stage for unprecedented prosperity—for a time. The eventual breakdown came not from honest acknowledgment of limitations, but from later generations failing to maintain this practice.

Teaching Without Idolizing: The Balance of Honor and Honesty

The greatest legacy mistake in organizational succession is transforming leaders into untouchable legends whose methods and decisions become beyond questioning. This mythologizing creates dysfunction that ripples through entire organizations and can persist for generations.

When leaders become untouchable icons, several damaging patterns emerge:

- ◆ Feedback stops—creating blind spots that grow increasingly dangerous over time
- ◆ Correction disappears—allowing small issues to develop into systemic problems
- ◆ Weakness becomes sacred—enshrining limitations as organizational culture rather than addressing them
- ◆ Innovation stagnates—as "what worked before" becomes the only acceptable approach

Missionpreneurs fundamentally refuse mythologized leadership in all its forms. Instead, they deliberately choose honest leadership that acknowledges both strengths and growth areas. This transparency creates psychological safety for emerging leaders to innovate without abandoning core values.

The next generation does not need untouchable heroes to emulate. They need authentic mentors who tell the truth about both successes and failures. This balanced approach provides both inspiration and practical guidance for navigating complex leadership challenges.

Final Test of Legacy Teaching: The Honest Assessment

Ask yourself honestly, with complete transparency:

If the next generation leads exactly as I do—with my blind spots, biases and weaknesses fully intact—would the mission be stronger or weaker five years from now? Ten years? Twenty?

That answer reveals whether true vision has been transferred to successors—or whether weakness has merely been reproduced and institutionalized. The distinction determines whether your organization will thrive or merely survive after your departure.

Closing Declaration

I was not called to create carbon copies of myself with all my limitations intact. I was called to cultivate leaders who exceed me in wisdom, impact, and organizational health. This is not a threat to my legacy but its fulfillment.

I choose honesty over ego protection. Growth over carefully managed image. Truth over comfortable illusions about my leadership. These choices require courage but deliver lasting impact.

I will teach vision clearly and comprehensively—ensuring core values and purpose remain uncompromised. Simultaneously, I will confront weakness courageously—in myself first, then in systems I've created that may perpetuate limitations.

Because true legacy is not what merely survives my leadership tenure. Legacy is what improves, expands, and flourishes after it.

The ultimate measure of my leadership is not what I built, but what others were empowered to build upon my foundation.

I am a Missionpreneur, and I pass strength forward without passing shadows. This is my commitment to those who will carry the vision beyond my season of leadership.

CHAPTER 20

MEASURING WHAT ACTUALLY MATTERS

Aligning Metrics With Legacy, Not Applause

What you measure determines what you multiply. This principle forms the foundation of sustainable business growth and meaningful impact. Organizations that measure the right things create systems that naturally reproduce those elements throughout their culture and operations.

Every organization, family, ministry, and leader is measuring something—whether intentionally or by default. Time. Money. Growth. Output. Reach. Results. These metrics shape decisions, priorities, and ultimately, the direction of your entire enterprise.

But legacy does not respond to attention.

It responds to alignment.

Missionpreneurs refuse to measure only what is visible, fast, or impressive. They measure what is formative, transferable, and eternal—because what you consistently measure is what your system quietly rewards. This deliberate approach to measurement creates accountability structures that reinforce your deepest values rather than merely chasing surface-level outcomes.

And what your system rewards eventually becomes your culture. This transformation happens gradually but inevitably, shaping not just what your organization does, but who your people become in the process.

The Limitation of Numbers

Numbers are not evil. They are useful. Quantitative metrics provide essential feedback for operational excellence and strategic decision-making.

They reveal activity.

They expose trends.

They help diagnose problems.

They inform tactical decisions.

But numbers are incomplete. They tell only part of the story—often the least significant part when building for generational impact. Relying exclusively on numerical metrics creates dangerous blind spots in your organizational vision.

Numbers cannot measure:

- Character
- Conviction

- Wisdom
- Faithfulness
- Integrity
- Obedience
- Spiritual authority
- Emotional maturity

The most important work of leadership happens beneath the surface. What is easiest to count is rarely what matters most. The transformative elements that create lasting impact often develop invisibly before manifesting in measurable outcomes.

Missionpreneurs understand this:

If you only measure outputs, you will eventually sacrifice outcomes that cannot be graphed. This trade-off may appear profitable in quarterly reports but proves devastating to long-term mission fulfillment.

When Metrics Become Masters

Metrics become dangerous when they stop informing leadership and start governing it. This shift represents a fundamental inversion of proper organizational hierarchy, where tools meant to serve the mission begin to define it instead.

This shift is subtle—and deadly. It rarely announces itself but gradually reshapes decision-making processes until values become secondary to visible results.

Metrics become masters when they:

- Replace discernment
- Justify compromise

♦ Drive decisions God was never invited into

♦ Redefine success by appearance instead of obedience

At that moment, leaders stop asking:

"Is this right?"

and start asking:

"Will this look successful?"

Missionpreneurs anchor every metric to mission, or they refuse to let it lead at all. They maintain this discipline even when it means slower growth, reduced visibility, or passing on opportunities that would boost impressive metrics at the expense of core values.

Biblical Measures of Success

Scripture rarely celebrates scale.

It celebrates faithfulness. This distinction provides a crucial corrective to contemporary business culture that often equates bigger with better and faster with more successful.

God measures:

♦ Endurance over excitement

♦ Obedience over applause

♦ Fruit over flash

♦ Multiplication over momentum

Jesus did not build the largest crowd.

He built the strongest disciples. His ministry strategy prioritized depth over breadth, investing intensively in relatively few people who would then transform their world.

The early church did not measure success by comfort, popularity, or cultural acceptance—but by faithfulness under pressure and multiplication through sacrifice. Their metrics focused on transformation rather than transaction, measuring changed lives rather than mere attendance.

God does not evaluate harvest by volume alone.

He evaluates the health of the seed and the condition of the soil. This holistic assessment examines not just results but the integrity of the process that produced them.

The False Security of Applause

Applause is one of the most unreliable metrics in leadership. External validation provides temporary encouragement but creates dangerous dependencies when used as a primary success indicator.

Crowds shift.

Culture changes.

Attention fades.

Public favor evaporates.

Leaders who build for applause drift when applause disappears. Without this external validation, they lose direction, confidence, and often their sense of purpose. This dependency creates organizational vulnerability to market fluctuations and public opinion.

Missionpreneurs build for fruit that remains long after attention moves on. They invest in outcomes that continue generating value regardless of recognition, creating sustainable impact that outlasts trends and transcends temporary accolades.

Applause celebrates moments.

Fruit reveals maturity. This distinction separates organizations built on performance from those built on purpose.

The Three Legacy Metrics

Missionpreneurs measure success across three primary domains—not instead of numbers, but above them. These qualitative metrics provide the framework within which quantitative measures find their proper context and meaning.

1. Formation

Who is becoming stronger, wiser, and more grounded? Formation focuses on the development of people—both leaders and those they serve—measuring growth in character, capacity, and conviction rather than merely tracking performance.

- Is character deepening?
- Are leaders maturing emotionally and spiritually?
- Are convictions steady under pressure?
- Is obedience shaping decision-making?

Growth without formation is inflation—not health. Organizations that expand without corresponding character development create hollow structures vulnerable to collapse under pressure or temptation.

2. Multiplication

Who is leading now—and who are they developing? Multiplication examines the organization's capacity to reproduce leadership at all levels, creating sustainable growth through intentional development rather than mere addition.

- ◆ Are leadership pipelines visible?
- ◆ Is authority being shared?
- ◆ Are apprentices becoming leaders?
- ◆ Is leadership reproducing itself?

If leadership stops with you, the mission stops with you. Multiplication ensures organizational continuity beyond any single leader's tenure, protecting the mission from personality dependency and enabling exponential rather than linear impact.

3. Durability

Would the mission survive pressure, transition, or loss? Durability measures organizational resilience—the capacity to maintain mission integrity through challenges, changes in leadership, and evolving external circumstances.

- ◆ Are systems functioning without constant oversight?
- ◆ Are values holding under stress?
- ◆ Could leadership change without chaos?

If success collapses when leadership changes, it was built on personality—not legacy. Durable organizations maintain momentum through transitions because their strength resides in systems and shared values rather than in charismatic individuals.

Any growth that weakens one of these three areas is not progress. It represents expansion at the expense of foundation—a dangerous trade that eventually undermines the entire enterprise.

Fruit Over Flash

Flash impresses quickly.

Fruit endures quietly. This distinction separates organizations building for immediate recognition from those investing in lasting transformation.

Fruit looks like:

♦ Restored families
♦ Stable leaders
♦ Wise decisions
♦ Consistent integrity
♦ Mature disciples
♦ Transferrable values

Fruit takes time.

But fruit survives seasons. Unlike flash that fades with changing conditions, fruit continues providing nourishment through fluctuating circumstances and challenging environments.

Missionpreneurs refuse to abandon fruit in pursuit of spectacle. They maintain patient commitment to developmental processes that yield lasting results, even when faster alternatives promise more immediate visibility or validation.

Measuring the Invisible

The most important indicators of legacy often cannot be charted. They exist in the realm of character, culture, and conviction—elements resistant to conventional measurement but essential to sustainable impact.

Ask questions numbers cannot answer:

- Are leaders making wise decisions without supervision?
- Is correction being received humbly?
- Is conflict being handled biblically?
- Are values enforced without escalation?
- Is humility increasing as influence expands?

These are signs of health.

And health always precedes multiplication. Organizations that prioritize these invisible indicators create the cultural conditions necessary for sustainable growth and lasting impact.

Accountability Without Idolatry

Missionpreneurs do not reject metrics.

They redeem them. Rather than abandoning measurement, they ensure metrics serve mission rather than replacing it, maintaining proper hierarchy between values and validation.

They track:

- Financial integrity
- Operational excellence
- Growth patterns
- Stewardship outcomes

But they refuse to worship numbers. This balanced approach maintains accountability without succumbing to the tyranny of metrics that sacrifice mission for measurables.

Numbers inform—but never override conscience.

Data supports—but never replaces discernment. This hierarchy ensures that quantitative feedback enhances rather than undermines mission fulfillment.

Any metric that pressures leaders to violate convictions has already exceeded its authority. When measurement systems create ethical compromise, they reveal themselves as false masters requiring immediate realignment with core values.

The Legacy Scorecard (Blueprint Section)

Rate each area from 1 (weak) to 5 (strong).

Formation

- ♦ Leaders show humility and courage
- ♦ Character precedes competence
- ♦ Faith governs decisions

Multiplication

- ♦ Leadership pipelines exist
- ♦ Authority is distributed
- ♦ Successors are visible

Durability

- ♦ Systems endure transition
- ♦ Values remain intact under pressure
- ♦ Mission survives without the founder

Any score below a 3 is not failure—but it is fragility. These vulnerable areas require intentional strengthening to prevent future collapse under pressure or during transition.

Fragility unaddressed becomes fracture. Organizational weaknesses do not resolve themselves but rather intensify over time unless deliberately remedied through strategic intervention and development.

The Temptation of Comparison

Comparison distorts measurement. It shifts focus from mission fulfillment to competitive positioning, replacing internal alignment with external validation as the primary success indicator.

When leaders measure success by:

- ♦ Size
- ♦ Speed
- ♦ Visibility
- ♦ Recognition

They abandon their assignment to chase someone else's. This mission drift occurs subtly as organizations gradually reorient around metrics that generate validation rather than impact, sacrificing unique calling for conventional recognition.

Missionpreneurs measure obedience, not proximity to peers. They maintain unwavering focus on their specific assignment, evaluating success by faithfulness to their unique calling rather than by comparison to others' achievements.

Calling is not competitive.

Assignment is not comparative. Each organization fulfills a distinct purpose that cannot be properly evaluated through external benchmarking.

The Long View

Legacy is rarely celebrated in real time. Its value emerges gradually as initial investments mature into lasting impact, often becoming fully visible only to future generations who benefit from present faithfulness.

It unfolds:

♦ Quietly

♦ Patiently

♦ Across generations

♦ In consistency, not moments

Missionpreneurs adopt a timeline longer than their own lifetime. They make decisions with multi-generational perspective, evaluating options based on long-term impact rather than immediate return.

They build for a future they may never see—but refuse to compromise the foundation of. This commitment to building beyond their own horizon creates organizational structures and cultural values capable of outlasting their founders.

Success Without Soul Is Failure

An organization can:

♦ Grow financially

♦ Expand influence

♦ Gain recognition

♦ Increase reach

And still fail. These external indicators of success provide incomplete assessment when separated from the internal integrity that gives them meaning and sustainability.

If success costs:

- ♦ Integrity
- ♦ Formation
- ♦ Faith
- ♦ Family
- ♦ Conscience

Then it is counterfeit—no matter how impressive it looks. True success maintains alignment between mission and methods, refusing achievement that undermines foundational values or compromises core identity.

Missionpreneurs would rather steward something faithful than scale something hollow. They prioritize depth over breadth, understanding that meaningful impact flows from integrity rather than from mere expansion.

Biblical Reflection — Noah

Noah measured obedience, not applause. His example provides powerful illustration of leadership guided by divine direction rather than public validation or conventional metrics of success.

He built faithfully for years without affirmation.

He endured ridicule without validation.

He followed instructions, not trends.

When the flood came, the numbers did not matter.

Alignment did. Noah's faithfulness to his assignment—regardless of external validation—positioned him to fulfill his purpose when circumstances validated his obedience.

Reflection Questions:

1. What am I currently measuring that may be driving performance—but not formation or faithfulness?
2. Which of the three legacy metrics—formation, multiplication, or durability—needs the most intentional attention right now?
3. If visibility, growth, or applause disappeared, what evidence would remain that this mission is still healthy?
4. What behaviors are my systems truly rewarding—and do they reflect my stated values or contradict them?
5. If I were removed tomorrow, what would continue to operate with clarity, integrity, and purpose—and what would collapse?

Closing Declaration

I will not measure success by applause.

I will not worship outcomes.

I will not sacrifice formation for speed.

I choose to measure what matters—

even when it is invisible, slow, and uncelebrated.

I steward obedience.

I protect formation.

I pursue multiplication that lasts.

I am a Missionpreneur, what I measure today determines what remains tomorrow.

CHAPTER 21

THE LEGACY EQUATION

Why the Mission Must Outlive the Moment

Winning is impressive.

Legacy is eternal.

History does not remember who started fast.

It remembers who finished faithful.

The world is full of people who were great once—

a season of momentum,

a moment of influence,

a short run of applause.

But very few build a legacy—something that outlives them. True legacy transcends individual achievement and becomes a foundation upon which others build their own success stories. It represents the culmination of purpose-driven decisions made consistently over time.

A legacy is not a highlight.

A legacy is a transfer.

Greatness ends when it stops inside you.

Legacy begins when it continues beyond you. When your vision, values, and methodologies become embedded in the operational DNA of those you've influenced, your impact extends far beyond your physical presence.

Anyone can build a moment people celebrate.

Only the called build a life that transforms generations. This distinction separates temporary success from enduring significance in the marketplace and beyond.

The Difference Between Success and Legacy

Success asks:

"How far can I go?" It measures achievement through personal milestones, revenue targets, and individual recognition within limited timeframes.

Legacy asks:

"How far can others go because I showed up?" It evaluates impact through the continued growth and development of people, organizations, and communities long after your direct involvement has ended.

Success says:

"Look at what I achieved." It centers attention on personal accomplishments and accolades that validate individual worth.

Legacy says:

"Look at who I built." It focuses on the development of capable leaders who carry forward mission-critical values and vision with their own unique strengths.

Success ends when you stop working.

Legacy lives on through people. When systems, cultures, and values you've established continue functioning effectively without your presence, you've created something truly sustainable.

The goal is not to die with accomplishments.

The goal is to leave people standing on top of your shoulders. This perspective transforms how we approach business development, team building, and strategic planning across every facet of our enterprise.

Success impresses crowds.

Legacy equips carriers. The former creates momentary admiration; the latter establishes generational impact through intentional investment in others.

Biblical Parallel — Abraham and Generational Impact

Abraham was not called to build a moment.

He was called to build generations. His covenant-based leadership model demonstrates how vision extends beyond immediate results to create lasting transformation.

God did not measure Abraham by:

- ♦ speed
- ♦ visibility

- popularity
- outcomes

God measured him by obedience and multiplication. These metrics transcend quarterly reports and annual reviews to establish a foundation for sustainable, long-term organizational health and mission fulfillment.

God didn't say:

"I will make your moment great."

He said:

"I will make your name great." This distinction highlights the difference between temporary recognition and enduring influence that shapes markets, communities, and individuals for generations.

Why?

Because Abraham's faith didn't terminate in himself.

It transferred. His leadership model wasn't designed for personal gratification but for generational transformation that continues to impact billions of people thousands of years later.

His obedience became infrastructure.

His faith became inheritance.

His calling became covenant. Each element represents a critical component of building an organization that outlasts its founder and continues delivering value through changing market conditions.

Legacy is not about living forever.

Legacy is about your mission living forever. This principle reshapes how we approach succession planning, knowledge transfer, and organizational development at every level of our enterprise.

Great Performers Think in Seasons — Legacy Builders Think in Generations

A performer asks:

"What can I accomplish this year?" Their horizon is limited to immediate results, quarterly targets, and annual reviews that validate short-term effectiveness.

A champion asks:

"What can I become over the next decade?" They focus on developing capabilities, systems, and relationships that create sustainable competitive advantage through changing market conditions.

A legacy builder asks:

"How will people be stronger 50 years from now because I lived aligned today?" This perspective transforms daily decisions into investments that compound over decades, creating exponential rather than linear impact.

Time destroys everything built on ego.

Time protects everything built on eternal purpose. Market trends change, technologies evolve, but purpose-driven organizations with clear values consistently outperform their competitors over extended timeframes.

Legacy is not created later.

Legacy is created now—

in how you make decisions,

how you treat people,

how you steward influence,

how you prepare successors. Each interaction, policy decision, and strategic initiative either contributes to or detracts from the lasting impact of your leadership.

The Legacy Equation

Legacy is not accidental.

Legacy is intentional. It requires systematic application of principles that transform fleeting success into lasting significance across every facet of business operations.

Here is the Legacy Equation:

Identity + Purpose + Discipline + Love = Legacy

Identity

Who you are when no one is watching.

Who you remain when the spotlight fades. This foundational element establishes the authentic character that withstands market pressures and maintains consistency through changing circumstances.

Purpose

The assignment that anchors your existence.

The reason you get up even when it's hard. This driving force aligns daily activities with long-term vision, ensuring resource allocation supports mission-critical objectives rather than merely responding to urgent demands.

Discipline

The daily choices that compound into greatness.

What you do consistently when motivation disappears. This operational excellence transforms inspirational vision into tangible results through systematic implementation of best practices regardless of emotional fluctuations.

Love

How people are strengthened because they encountered you.

How your leadership leaves others better, not smaller. This relational intelligence creates psychological safety, encourages innovation, and develops resilient teams capable of navigating complex challenges with integrity and mutual support.

Legacy is not what you build.

Legacy is what you build into people. The most valuable assets in any organization walk out the door every evening—investing in their development creates returns that continue generating value long after initial investments.

Remove any part of the equation—and legacy collapses. Each element reinforces the others, creating a synergistic impact greater than the sum of individual components when consistently applied throughout organizational systems.

Talent + attention + success $\neq$ legacy

Calling + consistency + compassion = legacy

The world does not need more stars.

It needs more builders of people. This principle reshapes recruitment, development, and advancement practices to prioritize capacity-building over credential-collecting.

Three Paths Every Leader Chooses

Every leader walks one of three paths—whether consciously or by default. These pathways determine not only personal fulfillment but organizational sustainability and market impact over extended timeframes.

✖ Path 1 — The Inward Path

All ambition. No contribution.

Wins alone. Dies alone.

Leaves impact only in memory, not movement. This approach creates temporary success that quickly dissipates when the leader departs, leaving organizational voids and succession challenges.

⚠ Path 2 — The Upward Path

Endless achievement chasing.

Always climbing. Never arriving.

Realizes too late that success didn't satisfy the soul. This trajectory creates impressive metrics but fails to develop sustainable systems that function effectively without constant leader intervention.

◌ Path 3 — The Outward Path

Uses excellence as a platform to elevate others.

Measures success by multiplication, not recognition.

Builds leaders instead of fans. This approach creates exponential impact through intentional development of others who continue advancing the mission with their own unique strengths and contributions.

The most fulfilled people are not those who were admired by many.

They are those who activated many. This distinction transforms how we measure success, allocate resources, and develop talent throughout our organizational ecosystem.

Legacy Requires Three Decisions

◯ Decision 1 — Use Your Gifts for Impact, Not Image

Stop obsessing over how your success looks.

Start obsessing over who your success helps. This shift redirects energy from impression management to value creation that solves meaningful problems for stakeholders, clients, and communities.

Image fades.

Impact compounds. While market perception matters, sustainable growth comes from consistently delivering transformative value rather than managing appearances. This principle guides marketing, communications, and brand development strategies.

◯ Decision 2 — Trade Attention for Contribution

Attention is loud but temporary.

Contribution is quiet but permanent. This perspective prioritizes meaningful value creation over visibility metrics that often distract from core mission objectives and organizational health indicators.

Applause does not raise leaders.

Investment does. Sustainable leadership development requires intentional resource allocation, systematic mentoring, and progressive responsibility rather than public recognition alone. This approach transforms how we identify, develop, and advance talent.

⬤ Decision 3 — Make the Mission Bigger Than the Moment

If the mission ends when applause ends, it was never a mission. True organizational purpose transcends market cycles, leadership transitions, and temporary setbacks to create lasting value for all stakeholders. This perspective guides strategic planning and resource allocation.

Legacy lives in people, not platforms.

In hearts, not headlines. While technology and systems matter, the most valuable organizational assets are the people who embody core values and advance the mission through changing circumstances and evolving market conditions.

Legacy Is Transfer — Who Are You Pouring Into?

Your legacy will not be determined by:

- ◆ how impressive you were
- ◆ how visible you became
- ◆ how celebrated you felt

It will be determined by:

- who you mentored
- who you developed
- who you challenged
- who became stronger because of you

The world does not change because someone is amazing.

The world changes because someone makes others amazing. This principle transforms leadership from performance to multiplication, creating exponential rather than linear impact through intentional investment in others.

Legacy does not ask,

"How impressive are you?"

It asks,

"Who is more capable because you lived?" This question reshapes performance metrics, development priorities, and strategic objectives throughout organizational systems and leadership practices.

Legacy Cannot Be Built in Isolation

You cannot build legacy alone. Sustainable impact requires collaborative relationships that provide accountability, perspective, and complementary strengths throughout the leadership journey.

You need:

- relationships
- accountability
- community

- mentors
- peers in the trenches

You were never designed to be a lone champion.

You were designed to be a builder of champions. This perspective transforms organizational structure from dependency hierarchies to empowerment networks that maximize collective impact through distributed leadership.

Isolation builds ego.

Community builds legacy. The most effective leaders create environments where shared wisdom, mutual support, and collaborative problem-solving accelerate mission fulfillment beyond what any individual could accomplish independently.

Legacy Outlasts the Body

One day:

- your name will stop trending
- your trophies will collect dust
- your audience will move on
- your career will end

But your impact doesn't have to. When properly developed, organizational systems, cultural values, and leadership pipelines continue functioning effectively long after founding leaders transition. This sustainability represents the ultimate measure of leadership effectiveness.

People do not live forever.

Purpose can. While individuals have limited lifespans, the missions and values they champion can continue transforming lives for generations when properly embedded in organizational DNA and successor development.

Your mortal life is temporary.

Your eternal impact is optional. This reality transforms daily decisions from short-term expediency to long-term significance, prioritizing sustainable value creation over temporary advantage.

Legacy is not automatic.

It is a decision. Intentional choices made consistently over time determine whether your leadership creates momentary success or lasting significance that continues generating value long after your direct involvement ends.

Reflection Questions

1. If your career ended tomorrow, what part of you would still be impacting people? Which systems, values, or practices would continue functioning effectively without your presence?

2. What do you want others to gain because you lived aligned with purpose? How can you structure your leadership approach to maximize this transfer of value?

3. Who is currently receiving your investment—and who should be? What strategic adjustments would optimize your leadership multiplication efforts?

4. What needs to change so your work serves people more than your ego? Which metrics or practices might be

redirecting your focus from lasting impact to temporary validation?

5. What is one action this week that contributes to legacy, not hype? How will you measure its effectiveness beyond immediate results?

Closing Declaration

I choose legacy over recognition.

I choose purpose over applause.

I choose transfer over attention.

I will not live only for moments.

I will build for generations.

My success will not stop with me.

My calling will not terminate in me.

My mission will outlive me.

I am a Missionpreneur. I live aligned. I build people. I finish faithful. Because the mission is bigger than the moment—and legacy begins now.

CHAPTER 22

LIVING FAITHFUL, NOT FAMOUS

Why Obedience Always Outlasts Applause

Every leader eventually stands at a crossroads where fundamental values are tested and long-term direction is determined. This moment of decision often arrives unexpectedly, sometimes disguised as opportunity, and invariably shapes the trajectory of both personal character and organizational legacy.

One road leads toward visibility, recognition, and applause. It promises immediate validation, external affirmation, and the intoxicating rush of public acknowledgment. The other leads toward obedience, surrender, and trust—a path marked by consistent alignment with core values regardless of external validation.

Both roads require sacrifice, though of dramatically different kinds. The path to recognition often demands compromise, constant performance, and the subtle erosion of foundational principles. The path of faithfulness requires ego surrender, patient endurance, and the courage to remain steadfast when no one is watching.

Missionpreneurs choose faithfulness—even when fame is available—because they recognize that lasting impact flows from consistent character rather than momentary acclaim. This deliberate choice shapes not only personal leadership but the entire organizational culture and legacy framework.

The Dangerous Allure of Recognition

Recognition is intoxicating in ways that often bypass our rational decision-making processes. It creates a neurological reward system that can gradually reshape our priorities without conscious awareness.

It validates effort, providing external confirmation that our work matters. It affirms sacrifice, suggesting that our personal costs have been worthwhile. It signals progress, offering tangible evidence of forward momentum. It feels like confirmation, wrapping us in the warm blanket of apparent success.

But recognition is a poor master, demanding increasing sacrifices while delivering diminishing returns. What begins as appreciation quickly transforms into addiction, requiring ever-larger doses to produce the same emotional response.

When applause becomes the reward, obedience quietly shifts. Leaders still do good things—but they begin doing them for the wrong reasons. Decisions become filtered through visibility instead of conviction. Strategy follows attention rather than purpose. Resource allocation favors what's seen over what's significant. The mission gradually morphs to accommodate whatever generates recognition.

Missionpreneurs refuse to let recognition redefine their assignment. They implement systems of accountability and regular purpose alignment reviews to ensure decisions remain anchored to mission rather than metrics of public approval.

They understand this truth: Applause never proves calling. It only exposes motive. The cheers of others reveal what we truly value, not what we're truly called to build.

Fame Is a Short-Term Metric

Fame measures:

◆ Visibility – how many see you in a moment
◆ Attention – how many listen temporarily
◆ Popularity – how many approve conditionally
◆ Cultural relevance – how well you align with current trends

Faithfulness measures:

◆ Obedience – consistent alignment with purpose and values
◆ Endurance – sustained commitment through changing seasons
◆ Integrity – wholeness between public actions and private decisions
◆ Alignment – congruence between stated mission and actual priorities

Fame fluctuates with trends, rising and falling with unpredictable market forces and shifting cultural appetites. Faithfulness anchors against them, providing stability through economic cycles, leadership transitions, and evolving business landscapes.

Fame is borrowed from people who can reclaim it at any moment based on changing preferences or perceived missteps. Faithfulness is entrusted by God as an internal compass that functions regardless of external circumstances or public opinion.

One expires quickly, often disappearing faster than it arrived and leaving little substance in its wake. The other echoes eternally, creating ripple effects of impact that continue long after the initial actions are forgotten.

The Quiet Power of Obedience

Obedience rarely looks impressive in the moment. It lacks the dramatic flair that captures attention and generates immediate results. Instead, it builds slowly, consistently, and often invisibly—creating foundations that support lasting impact.

It often looks like:

- Saying no when opportunity is available but misaligned with core mission
- Waiting while others pass you, maintaining patience during preparation seasons
- Staying hidden when exposure is offered but premature for your development
- Choosing integrity over advancement when shortcuts present themselves

◆ Leading consistently when no one is watching or acknowledging your efforts

Obedience does not build applause. It builds trust—first with God, then with people. This trust becomes the foundation for sustainable influence that outlasts trends and survives scrutiny. While applause creates momentary connection, trust creates lasting relationship.

Missionpreneurs understand: God does not reward visibility. He rewards faithfulness. The metrics that matter most are rarely captured in analytics dashboards or social media engagement rates. They're measured in lives changed, values transmitted, and mission sustained.

When Obedience Costs You

True obedience always costs something. The price tag attached to alignment is rarely small and never negotiable. These costs represent the true investment in legacy-level leadership.

It may cost:

◆ Speed – moving at the pace of wisdom rather than opportunity

◆ Position – accepting assignments that feel beneath your capabilities

◆ Influence – releasing platforms that compromise your values

◆ Approval – making unpopular decisions that honor long-term mission

◆ Invitations – missing "networking opportunities" that would dilute focus

◆ Reputation – being misunderstood by those who measure by different metrics

Missionpreneurs do not interpret this cost as punishment. They recognize it as preparation. Each sacrifice becomes part of the formation process that builds capacity for greater responsibility and sustainable impact.

What God withholds in one season often protects what He plans to entrust in another. What feels like loss now may be preservation later. The opportunities declined, the shortcuts avoided, and the integrity maintained all contribute to a foundation that can sustain genuine, lasting influence.

Short-term obedience guards long-term authority. The temporary losses create space for permanent gains that cannot be achieved through shortcuts or compromise. This economy of faithfulness operates on principles that contradict conventional business wisdom but produce results that outlast conventional business success.

Biblical Parallel — John the Baptist

John the Baptist had influence that extended to the highest levels of society and the farthest reaches of his region. He had a following that grew daily as people recognized the authenticity and power of his message. He had momentum that positioned him as a major religious and cultural figure of his time.

Then Jesus arrived—and John stepped aside with immediate and complete clarity about his role. This transition moment reveals the heart of faithful leadership in action.

He didn't compete for audience share or attempt to maintain his position. He didn't cling to the platform he had built through years of sacrifice and discipline. He didn't protect his platform or negotiate a partnership arrangement to preserve his influence.

He said, "He must increase, and I must decrease." This simple statement represents the most profound leadership transition in history—a voluntary release of influence at the height of effectiveness.

That is legacy-level obedience. It demonstrates the courage to recognize when your role is changing and the humility to embrace that change without resistance.

John's name faded from public attention as Jesus' ministry expanded. His impact did not. The foundation he laid became essential to the mission that followed, and his example of faithful obedience continues to instruct leaders thousands of years later.

The Final Transfer of Control

Every Missionpreneur eventually reaches a moment of surrender where theoretical trust becomes practical release. This crucible experience transforms intellectual commitment into lived reality.

A moment where you must release:

- Outcomes – the specific results of your obedience
- Reputation – how others perceive and describe your work
- Recognition – whether your contribution is acknowledged

- Timing – when your investment will produce visible returns

This is not resignation that abandons responsibility. It is alignment that acknowledges ultimate authority. The difference is profound—one leads to disengagement while the other leads to empowerment.

You stop trying to control legacy and start trusting God with it. This shift transforms the leadership burden from crushing to sustainable. Instead of carrying the weight of results, you carry the responsibility of faithfulness—a much lighter load that produces greater results.

Legacy is not built by clinging to control, recognition, or authority. It is built by releasing these natural desires in exchange for something greater. What appears to be surrender becomes the very mechanism of enduring impact.

Why Faithful Leaders Are Remembered Longer

Famous leaders are remembered for moments—specific achievements, quotable statements, or visible victories. Faithful leaders are remembered for impact—the transformed lives, sustained values, and continued mission that outlasts their direct involvement.

Faithful leaders:

- Built others quietly, investing in people without demanding credit
- Spoke truth consistently, maintaining the same message in public and private

- ◆ Corrected lovingly, addressing issues without destroying people
- ◆ Modeled humility visibly, demonstrating the values they proclaimed
- ◆ Chose alignment privately, making unseen decisions that honored their mission

Their names may fade from organizational histories and public recognition. But their influence multiplies through the leaders they developed, the values they instilled, and the systems they established with integrity.

Time forgets hype, erasing even the most celebrated achievements that lack substance. Time honors faithfulness, preserving and amplifying impact that flows from consistent character and aligned action.

The Measure of a Finish

A strong finish is not loud, accompanied by fanfare and public accolades. It is stable, marked by sustainable systems, healthy relationships, and transferred values that continue after direct leadership ends.

Missionpreneurs finish well when:

- ◆ Successors are prepared through intentional development and genuine empowerment
- ◆ Systems endure because they're built on principles rather than personalities
- ◆ Families remain intact, having been prioritized alongside professional pursuits

♦ Faith remains central, continuing as the foundation for decisions and direction

♦ The mission survives them, continuing with renewed energy and expanding impact

A faithful finish validates a faithful life. The end of active leadership becomes the most revealing measure of what was actually built during the journey. What remains when position and authority are removed reveals what was truly constructed beyond personal platform.

The Legacy You Will Never See

Some of the greatest outcomes of obedience:

♦ Are delayed, emerging years or decades after the initial investment

♦ Are hidden, occurring in contexts you'll never directly observe

♦ Are realized in future generations, manifesting in people you'll never meet

Missionpreneurs do not demand visibility as proof of impact. They trust God with the harvest—even when they never see it. This faith-driven perspective allows them to make decisions based on alignment rather than immediate results, investing in outcomes that may only become visible long after their direct involvement has ended.

You may never know who was strengthened because you stayed obedient when compromise seemed reasonable. You may never hear the story of who was protected because you said no when saying yes would have been personally beneficial. The full impact of faithful leadership extends far beyond measurable metrics.

But God knows each life touched, each value transmitted, and each ripple effect created. And that is enough to sustain commitment when visible results are scarce and immediate feedback is absent.

The Dangerous Question of "What If"

"What if this makes me known?" whispers the desire for recognition that lives in every leader. "What if this grows my platform?" suggests the ambition that masquerades as strategic thinking. "What if this elevates my name?" asks the ego that seeks validation through visibility.

Missionpreneurs ask a better question that reorients perspective and purifies motive. A question that transforms decision-making at its foundation.

"What if this strengthens what remains when I'm gone?" This forward-looking perspective evaluates opportunities not by immediate benefit but by lasting contribution to mission sustainability.

That question transforms ambition into obedience. It filters opportunities through legacy rather than leverage, ensuring that each decision contributes to lasting impact rather than temporary advantage.

The Final Legacy Choice

At the end of the road, you will not be judged by:

- The size of your platform or how many followed your content
- The reach of your influence or how many knew your ideas
- The number of people who knew your name or recognized your brand

You will be judged by what you built into others—the character you helped form, the values you helped instill, and the mission you helped advance through your consistent investment in people and principles.

You can build:

- A name that generates recognition and opens doors
- A brand that creates value and captures attention
- A moment that shines brightly but burns quickly

Or you can build:

- People who carry values forward and multiply impact
- Systems that sustain mission beyond your direct involvement
- Faith that anchors decisions in timeless principles

Platforms fade with changing technologies and shifting attention spans. People endure, transmitting values and continuing mission through relationships that transcend trends and survive transitions.

The Missionpreneur Commitment

Living faithful is a daily decision, not a one-time declaration. It requires consistent recommitment as challenges arise, opportunities appear, and circumstances change.

A commitment:

♦ To obedience over ego, choosing alignment even when it costs visibility

♦ To stewardship over spotlight, managing resources for mission rather than recognition

♦ To endurance over escape, remaining faithful when difficulty would justify departure

♦ To truth over trend, standing firm when cultural currents push against values

♦ To formation over fame, prioritizing character development over platform building

It is not glamorous, offering few moments of public celebration or external validation. It is not celebrated, often going unnoticed by those who measure by different metrics. It is not fast, requiring patient investment in outcomes that develop slowly.

It is eternal. The impact of faithful leadership continues long after platforms disappear and recognition fades, creating legacies that outlast lifetimes and influence generations.

Final Reflection Questions

1. Where in your life is recognition tempting you to compromise obedience? What specific decisions are

being influenced by the desire for visibility or validation?

2. What decision would look different if faithfulness—not visibility—was your metric? How would your current priorities shift if legacy impact rather than immediate recognition guided your choices?

3. What are you currently stewarding that you may never receive credit for? How does this hidden investment contribute to your larger mission?

4. What would it look like to trust God with outcomes instead of managing your image? What specific control mechanisms would you need to release?

5. How do you want people to be stronger because you lived obediently? What specific character qualities or values do you hope to transmit to those you influence?

Closing Declaration

I was never called to be famous. I was called to be faithful. This commitment guides every business decision and strategic direction within our family holding company, ensuring our actions align with our deepest values and long-term vision.

I choose obedience over ego. I choose surrender over applause. I choose trust over recognition. These principles form the foundation of our business philosophy, creating a legacy-minded approach that prioritizes sustainable impact over short-term gains.

Fame fades. Faithfulness multiplies. Legacy remains. In the marketplace where trends come and go, we build enterprises designed to weather economic cycles and create intergenerational value through consistent, principled leadership.

I am a Missionpreneur. I live aligned. I finish faithful. This identity shapes how we evaluate opportunities, develop partnerships, and measure success—not merely by financial metrics, but by alignment with our God-given purpose and mission.

And what I build will outlive me—not because my name is attached to it, but because God's fingerprints are all over it.

CONCLUSION

THE WORK THAT CONTINUES AFTER YOU

If you have read this far, one truth should now be unmistakable: Legacy is not something you contemplate in your later years or address when convenient. It is a foundational principle that must be woven into every business decision, family conversation, and strategic initiative you undertake today. The choices you make now—whether deliberate or unconscious—are already forming the framework of what will remain.

This book was never intended to provide momentary inspiration or a temporary surge of motivation. Rather, it was meticulously crafted to provoke permanent alignment between your daily actions and your generational vision. The principles outlined here are designed to transform how you approach leadership, ownership, and the stewardship of what has been entrusted to you.

Because legacy does not respond to good intentions or occasional efforts. It responds only to consistent obedience, intentional structure, and faithful stewardship demonstrated over time. The systems you implement today become the safeguards of tomorrow. The boundaries you establish now become the guidelines that future generations will follow.

What you tolerate today—whether mediocrity, misalignment, or mission drift—inevitably becomes embedded in your organizational culture tomorrow. What you take time to clarify today—values, expectations, and processes—creates stability and confidence for those who follow. What you delay addressing today—difficult conversations, necessary transitions, or structural weaknesses—will invariably emerge as conflict and crisis for your successors.

Legacy is already forming in your family, your business, and your ministry. The only question that remains is whether it is forming by deliberate design or by unconscious default. The choice to be intentional is yours alone to make.

From Information to Implementation

Knowledge alone, no matter how profound, does not secure legacy. Application—consistent, disciplined implementation—is what transforms principles into lasting impact. Information without action creates informed failures, not enduring successes.

Many leaders already know what should be done to secure their legacy:

♦ Values should be clearly articulated and documented

- ◆ Family roles and responsibilities should be explicitly defined
- ◆ Operational systems should be thoroughly documented and transferable
- ◆ Authority should be thoughtfully distributed across capable leaders
- ◆ Succession should be prepared for well in advance of necessity

Yet far fewer leaders pause long enough in their busy schedules to establish order around their vision. They remain perpetually caught in the urgent cycle of daily operations, never creating the infrastructure that would allow their mission to outlive their personal involvement.

This book was written to help you cross that critical line—from intellectual agreement to decisive action, from momentary insight to enduring infrastructure, from leadership centered exclusively on your capabilities to leadership built to thrive beyond your presence. It provides both the framework and the motivation to move from good intentions to concrete implementation.

Legacy truly begins the moment your vision becomes executable without your physical presence or constant intervention. When others can carry forward the mission with clarity and confidence because you've created systems that transcend personality, you have begun to build something that will outlast you.

The Real Work of a Missionpreneur

Missionpreneurs consistently do the work others postpone. They recognize that short-term discomfort creates long-term stability. They understand that today's discipline becomes tomorrow's freedom.

They initiate difficult conversations early, addressing potential issues before they become entrenched problems. They confront tension directly and constructively before it fractures important relationships. They choose obedience to their calling over pursuing every attractive opportunity that arises. They invest time and resources to build robust systems when it would be easier to rely solely on their personal charisma or individual capabilities.

They accept a truth many leaders avoid or deny: If your organization, family enterprise, or ministry cannot function effectively without your constant presence, it is not yet finished. It remains incomplete—a work dependent on a single point of failure rather than a sustainable legacy.

The dependence of others often feels validating to a leader's ego. There is a certain satisfaction in being needed, in having others seek your approval or direction for every decision. But genuine legacy requires progressive release—the gradual, intentional transfer of knowledge, authority, and responsibility to those who will carry the mission forward.

Legacy Requires Courage

Building legacy demands extraordinary courage in specific areas where most leaders struggle:

- Stepping out of the spotlight intentionally, even when you could retain center stage
- Releasing authority before it is demanded or circumstances force your hand
- Allowing others to lead differently than you would, honoring their unique gifts and approaches
- Admitting blind spots and weaknesses without defensiveness or justification
- Submitting personal ambition to the greater calling of obedience and stewardship

These acts of courage may feel uncomfortable or even counterintuitive in the moment. Yet courage demonstrated now prevents organizational collapse later. The temporary vulnerability of honest assessment creates lasting strength. The momentary discomfort of releasing control builds sustainable leadership capacity throughout your organization.

Legacy leadership is never about protecting ego or personal reputation. It is fundamentally about protecting and nurturing what God has entrusted to your care—people, resources, mission, and vision. The focus shifts from personal achievement to faithful stewardship.

What feels uncomfortable or challenging today— documentation, delegation, development of others—becomes a protective shield for your mission tomorrow. The systems that seem tedious to create now will preserve your values when you are no longer present to articulate them.

The Generational View

Most people build for seasons—focusing on quarterly results, annual goals, or five-year plans. Missionpreneurs, by contrast, build for generations. They maintain awareness of immediate objectives while simultaneously considering how today's decisions will impact those who follow decades from now.

They understand fundamental truths that shape their approach to legacy:

◆ Families outlast companies—relationships endure beyond business entities

◆ Values outlive strategies—what you believe matters more than what you do

◆ Systems protect what passion alone cannot—documented processes preserve wisdom

◆ Faith sustains what talent initiates—spiritual foundation provides enduring strength

What you establish today—whether principles, processes, or precedents—becomes someone else's starting line tomorrow. The boundaries you define, the culture you cultivate, and the expectations you normalize will shape how future generations approach the mission you began.

You are not building primarily for immediate recognition or applause. You are building for multi-generational endurance—creating something that will stand firm through challenges you cannot foresee and opportunities you will not personally witness. This perspective transforms daily decisions from tactical reactions to strategic investments in future impact.

What Remains When You Are Gone

One day, inevitably, your voice will fall silent in rooms you currently lead. Your physical presence will no longer guide decisions, resolve conflicts, or inspire action. This reality is not morbid; it is motivational—compelling you to prepare thoroughly for the continuation of what matters most.

When that transition occurs, what will speak in your absence?

- Will clearly articulated values still govern critical decisions?
- Will developed leaders act with the courage and wisdom you've modeled?
- Will faith still anchor organizational culture and family identity?
- Will the mission continue without constant explanation or reinforcement?

The answers to these crucial questions are not determined later, when succession becomes urgent or transition is forced by circumstances. They are being written now—through your priorities, your investments, your documentation, and your development of others. Every system you create, every value you clarify, and every leader you develop is answering these questions in advance.

Faithfulness Is the Final Metric

Our culture typically celebrates the visible, the viral, and the momentarily significant. History tends to remember the loud, the disruptive, and those who captured public attention. But Heaven honors the faithful—those who stewarded well what was entrusted to them, regardless of recognition.

For the missionpreneur, the goal was never primarily to be known, recognized, or celebrated. It was to be obedient—to fulfill the specific calling placed on your life and to steward the resources, relationships, and opportunities you were given with integrity and purpose.

Missionpreneurs understand that God does not ultimately ask how visible you became, how large your organization grew, or how impressive your achievements appeared. He asks how faithfully you stewarded what was entrusted specifically to you—whether that was much or little by worldly standards.

When all external measurements end—market share, revenue growth, social media influence—faithfulness remains as the enduring metric. It is the standard that transcends time and circumstance, the one evaluation that matters beyond all others.

A Lasting Charge

If you do only one thing after closing this book, let it be this: Choose clarity over comfort in every aspect of your legacy journey. Embrace the temporary discomfort of definition over the permanent damage of ambiguity.

Write things down—document your values, vision, and expectations explicitly. Have the conversations—address succession, authority, and future transitions directly. Define the roles—clarify who is responsible for what, both now and in transition periods. Build the systems—create processes that can function without your constant oversight. Prepare the people—

invest intentionally in developing those who will carry the mission forward. Anchor everything in faith—ensure spiritual foundation underlies all structural elements.

Legacy rarely breaks because leaders fail catastrophically. More often, it breaks because leaders delay addressing critical issues until time runs out. They postpone difficult conversations, avoid documentation, and neglect systematic development of successors until transition becomes urgent rather than intentional. Procrastination, not incompetence, is legacy's most common enemy.

The Mission Continues

Angeron & Melvin Legacy Holdings, LLC was not established merely to manage assets or generate financial returns. It was purposefully built to model intentional legacy construction—faith-anchored, people-centered, and generationally aligned. Our structure, processes, and decisions are designed to demonstrate principles that transcend our specific circumstances.

This book exists for the same fundamental reason. It was not created to elevate a name or build personal recognition. Rather, it was written to strengthen a mission—to provide practical guidance for those committed to building legacies that honor God and serve generations beyond their lifetime. It represents our commitment to steward not only our own legacy but to help others develop theirs.

And now, the work moves to you. The principles have been shared, the framework established, and the challenge issued. The responsibility for implementation—for transforming concept into reality in your unique context—rests in your hands.

Final Declaration

You were not entrusted with influence, resources, and opportunity merely for personal success or temporary achievement. You were entrusted with these gifts for generational impact—to create ripples of positive change that continue long after your direct involvement ends.

Build what outlives you—structures, systems, and values that transcend your personal presence. Prepare those who come after you—investing generously in their development without expectation of control. Walk obediently each day—even when your faithfulness goes unrecognized and your sacrifice remains unseen.

Because long after titles fade and applause stops, legacy will still be speaking through the lives you've influenced and the systems you've established. Your impact will continue through generations you will never meet and circumstances you cannot foresee.

And the greatest legacy a Missionpreneur can leave is this:

When I stepped away, what God entrusted to me grew stronger.

THE MISSIONPRENEUR LIFE

Living called. Leading boldly. Finishing well.

You've read the pages. You've absorbed the mindset. You've seen the framework. You've looked in the mirror. This journey has taken you through the essential elements of what it means to live with purpose and lead with conviction in today's complex business landscape.

You've been stretched, challenged, and sharpened through each concept and principle we've explored together. The frameworks and strategies presented weren't merely theoretical—they were battle-tested approaches designed to transform how you view your mission and purpose.

But now comes the moment that separates information from transformation: The critical juncture where knowledge must transition into deliberate action. This is where most aspiring leaders falter, collecting insights without implementing them.

What will you do with what you now know?

This book was not written to hype you up. It was written to wake you up. To cut through the noise and reconnect you with your core purpose and calling as a missionpreneur who creates lasting impact.

Not to convince you that you are strong—but to remind you that you have always been strong. Your resilience has been within you, waiting to be channeled toward your highest calling and most meaningful work.

Not to make you fearless—but to prove that fear was never your master. Fear may be present, but it need not dictate your decisions or diminish your boldness in pursuing what matters most.

Not to make you ready—but to reveal that you have been ready for a long time. The preparation phase is complete; the implementation phase begins now, with clarity and conviction guiding your steps forward.

What you needed was never permission. What you needed was clarity. The kind of strategic clarity that eliminates confusion, silences distractions, and illuminates the path of highest contribution.

And now, you have it. You possess the mindset, the framework, and the strategic direction to move forward with confidence and purpose.

You Now Know the Truth About Greatness

Greatness is no longer a mystery to be chased or a distant goal to be admired. It has been demystified through the principles we've examined and the frameworks we've established.

It is not luck. It is not genetics. It is not popularity. It is not adrenaline. It is not hype. It is not talent alone. These are the false currencies that many trade in, but they never deliver lasting significance or impact.

Greatness is alignment over insecurity. Calling over comparison. Identity over approval. Consistency over emotion. Discipline over excitement. Endurance over comfort. Purpose over applause. Legacy over spotlight. These are the true exchanges that produce extraordinary outcomes and generational impact.

This book was not written to make you someone else. It was written to make you fully you. To strip away the accumulated layers of conformity and expectation that have masked your authentic voice and vision.

The world does not need another copy. It needs your original calling, lived with conviction. Your unique perspective, approach, and solution are precisely what your market, community, and industry require—not a replica of someone else's success formula.

You're Not at the End — You're at the Beginning

Some people finish a book and say, "That was inspiring." They close the pages and return to business as usual, momentarily motivated but ultimately unchanged.

Missionpreneurs finish a book and say, "It's time to get to work." They recognize that true value comes not from consumption but from implementation—turning insights into initiatives and concepts into concrete actions.

Nothing in your life changes until your identity takes control of your habits. Nothing in your work rises until your discipline becomes non-negotiable. Nothing in your calling manifests until purpose becomes your priority. These are the fundamental shifts that transform potential into performance and vision into visible impact.

You are not waiting on destiny. Destiny has been waiting on you. The opportunities, impact, and legacy you're meant to create have been patiently awaiting your decision to step fully into your calling with clarity and commitment.

There is a stronger, steadier, more disciplined, more grounded version of you ready to lead. This version has been developing beneath the surface, gaining strength through every challenge, setback, and victory you've experienced.

That version no longer lives in the shadows. The time for hesitation, second-guessing, and playing small has passed. Your full potential demands expression.

It's time for them to take command. For your highest self to direct your daily decisions, strategic priorities, and leadership approach.

Your Life Is No Longer About Proving — It's About Becoming

You don't have to fight for approval anymore. You don't have to chase validation anymore. You don't have to earn worth anymore. These exhausting cycles of performance and validation seeking can finally end.

From this point forward:

Your worth is settled. Your identity is secure. Your confidence is anchored. Your calling is not negotiable. These foundational truths liberate you to lead from a place of abundance rather than scarcity, conviction rather than insecurity.

You are no longer performing to deserve value. You are performing to deliver value. This fundamental shift transforms how you approach your work, your relationships, and your mission in the marketplace.

That shift changes everything. It alters how you make decisions, allocate resources, build teams, create offerings, and measure success. Purpose rather than approval becomes your primary metric for evaluating opportunities and initiatives.

Yes, It Will Be Hard — and Yes, You Can Handle Hard

Let's be honest. Honesty serves us better than false optimism or unrealistic expectations about the path ahead.

Living aligned is not the easiest path. It demands more from you than the path of least resistance or the road of conformity that many choose by default.

There will be days when:

- emotions try to lead
- pressure feels heavy
- doubt resurfaces
- excuses whisper
- fear knocks
- people misunderstand you
- progress feels slow
- obedience feels quiet

That is not failure. That is confirmation. These challenges are not evidence that you're on the wrong path—they're confirmation that you're on the right one. The path of significance is never without resistance.

If destiny were effortless, everyone would step into it. The fact that it demands your full engagement, resilience, and commitment is precisely what makes it valuable and what ensures that only the determined few will fully realize it.

You are not called to the easy path. You are called to the meaningful path. The path that creates lasting value, solves significant problems, and leaves an indelible mark on those you serve.

And meaningful demands strength. Not just occasional bursts of energy or enthusiasm, but sustained strength—the kind that shows up daily, remains consistent through challenges, and endures beyond initial excitement.

Strength is no longer your question. It is now your resource. You don't need to wonder if you have what it takes; you need only to access and deploy the strength that has been cultivated through every previous challenge you've overcome.

How You'll Know the Missionpreneur Mindset Is Working

Not when things get easy. But when things get hard—and you don't fold. When obstacles arise and you meet them with steady resolve rather than reactivity or retreat.

You'll notice that discipline stops feeling optional. Pressure no longer intimidates you. Confidence appears before results. Emotions lose their authority. Chaos no longer steals focus. Setbacks don't dismantle belief. Applause doesn't inflate ego. Silence doesn't threaten identity. Success doesn't distract you from purpose.

One day, you'll quietly realize: Nothing can stop me unless I let it. This realization doesn't come with fanfare or external validation—it emerges as a quiet certainty that fundamentally alters how you approach every challenge.

That is the moment you become unstoppable. Not because circumstances bow to your will, but because your resolve no longer bows to circumstances. Your commitment to your calling transcends conditions, convenience, and comfort.

Your Calling Is Bigger Than You

Your calling is not primarily about:

- ♦ income
- ♦ platform

- performance
- reputation
- recognition

While these may be byproducts of living aligned with your purpose, they are not the purpose itself. They make poor primary motivations and inevitably lead to disillusionment when prioritized above impact.

Your calling is about:

- who you lift
- who you sharpen
- who you empower
- who becomes more because of you

These are the true metrics of significance—the ripple effects of your leadership that extend far beyond your immediate reach or recognition. Your greatest contributions may never be directly attributed to you.

A Missionpreneur does not walk into rooms asking, "How can I win?" This self-centered approach limits potential and restricts impact to what you alone can achieve.

A Missionpreneur walks in asking, "How can we rise?" This collaborative, abundance-minded approach multiplies impact by engaging others in a shared mission that transcends individual achievement.

That mindset does not just change outcomes. It changes generations. It creates legacy impact that continues long after your direct involvement ends, establishing patterns, principles, and possibilities that benefit those who come after you.

The Missionpreneur Code

Let these words anchor how you live from this point forward. They form not just a philosophy but a practical operating system for daily decision-making and leadership:

I don't chase hype — I chase purpose. The fleeting excitement of trends and temporary acclaim holds no appeal compared to the enduring satisfaction of meaningful contribution.

I don't perform for approval — I perform from identity. My work flows from who I am, not from what others expect or demand. This internal alignment produces external excellence.

I don't panic under pressure — I activate under pressure. Challenges don't diminish me; they reveal my capacity and clarify my priorities. Pressure becomes a catalyst rather than a constraint.

I don't quit when it gets hard — I rise when it gets hard. Difficulty is not a signal to retreat but an invitation to advance with greater determination and creative problem-solving.

I don't build moments — I build legacy. My focus extends beyond immediate results to generational impact. Every decision is evaluated through the lens of lasting significance rather than temporary success.

If this resonates, it's because it was already inside you. This book did not create it. It unlocked it. These principles aren't foreign concepts being imposed but dormant truths being awakened.

This Is Not Goodbye — It's Activation

You have the mindset. You have the identity. You have the structure. You have the clarity. You have the calling. The essential elements are in place for transformative action and impact.

Now you have a decision. Not a complex one with numerous options, but a binary choice: Will you implement or will you hesitate? Will you advance or will you retreat?

Will you live what you now know? Will you translate awareness into action, insights into implementation, and concepts into concrete steps forward?

Because if you do:

♦ your life will rise

♦ your leadership will rise

♦ your family will rise

♦ your circle will rise

♦ your future will rise

Not because you are lucky—but because you are aligned. Alignment with your purpose, values, and calling creates a momentum that mere circumstance or coincidence never could. It positions you to maximize opportunities and navigate challenges with wisdom and resilience.

A Final Charge

You did not find this book by accident. You did not finish this book by accident. You are not reading these words by accident. There is intentionality in this moment that transcends mere coincidence.

You are a leader—even if you still feel unfinished. Your influence doesn't await perfection; it requires only your willingness to step forward with what you currently possess.

You are a builder—even if you are still learning. The most significant structures are built by those who continue to develop their skills throughout the construction process.

You are chosen—even if doubt visits occasionally. Your moments of uncertainty don't negate your calling; they humanize it and keep you dependent on wisdom beyond your own.

You are called—even if others don't see it yet. External validation may follow your obedience, but it should never precede it. Move forward with or without the affirmation of others.

There is something powerful inside you. And the world is waiting to experience it. Your unique combination of perspective, skills, experiences, and vision has prepared you to meet specific needs that others cannot address in precisely the same way.

Not someday. Not when conditions are perfect. Not when everything feels safe. These are the procrastinator's excuses that have kept too many missions unrealized and too many callings unfulfilled.

Now.

The mission does not start later. The mission starts today. With whatever resources you currently have, whatever clarity you've gained, and whatever courage you can summon.

Turn the page in your life. Step into alignment. Show up on purpose. Lead boldly. Build what outlives you. These aren't merely inspirational phrases but practical imperatives—the essential actions that transform vision into reality.

Right here. Right now. For the rest of your life. Not as a temporary experiment or short-term initiative, but as a fundamental reorientation of how you approach every day, decision, and opportunity.

Because you already know the truth:

You were built for more. You were built to lead. You were built to finish well. These aren't grandiose claims but sober recognitions of the potential and purpose that have been woven into your very identity.

And now—more than ever—the world needs what's inside you. The problems awaiting solutions, the people awaiting leadership, and the possibilities awaiting activation depend on your willingness to step fully into your calling.

Go live the mission.

www.ingramcontent.com/pod-product-compliance
Lightning Source LLC
Chambersburg PA
CBHW060408130626
46555CB00005B/2007